The Fall of the
Berlin Wall

The Fall of the Berlin Wall

REASSESSING THE CAUSES AND CONSEQUENCES OF THE END OF THE COLD WAR

Edited by

Peter Schweizer

HOOVER INSTITUTION PRESS
STANFORD UNIVERSITY
Stanford, California

WILLIAM J. CASEY INSTITUTE
OF THE CENTER FOR SECURITY POLICY
Washington, D.C.

www-hoover.stanford.edu

Hoover Institution Press Publication No. 474

First printing, 2000
06 05 04 03 02 01 00   9 8 7 6 5 4 3 2

Manufactured in the United States of America
The paper used in this publication meets the minimum requirements
of American National Standard for Information Sciences—Permanence
of Paper for Printed Library Materials, ANSI Z39.48–1984. ⊗

Cover photo credits: President Reagan delivers his Berlin address in front of the
Brandenburg Gate, June 12, 1987; Reagan appealed to Soviet leader Mikhail
Gorbachev to dismantle the Berlin Wall (Corbis/Bettman; all rights reserved).
A break in the Berlin Wall, November 12, 1989
(AP/Wide World Photos/John Gaps III; all rights reserved).

Library of Congress Cataloging-in-Publication Data
The fall of the Berlin Wall : reassessing the causes and consequences of the end of
the Cold War / edited by Peter Schweizer.
    p.   cm.
Papers presented at a symposium held Feb. 22, 1999, in Washington, D.C.
Includes bibliographical references.
ISBN 0-8179-9822-5 (alk. paper)
    1. World politics—1985–1995—Congresses.   2. Cold War—Congresses.
3. Berlin Wall, Berlin, Germany, 1961–1989—Congresses.   4. United States—
Foreign relations—1981–1989—Congresses.   5. United States—Foreign relations—
Soviet Union—Congresses.   6. Soviet Union—Foreign relations—United States—
Congresses.   7. Reagan, Ronald—Congresses.   I. Schweizer, Peter, 1964–
D849.F35   2000
327.73047–dc21
                                                                99-048947
                                                                CIP

CONTENTS

FOREWORD

THIS YEAR marks the tenth anniversary of the fall of the Berlin Wall, perhaps the most potent symbol of the Cold War.

To commemorate that historic event, and to further understand the U.S. policies and actions that preceded it, the Hoover Institution cosponsored a symposium entitled "The Fall of the Berlin Wall: Reassessing the Causes and Consequences of the End of the Cold War" with the William J. Casey Institute of the Center for Security Policy. The symposium brought together several individuals who played pivotal roles in shaping American Cold War policy during the 1980s. Some of the participants not only served in the Reagan administration but have a long association with the Hoover Institution and the Center for Security Policy.

Comments by the participants provided an important window on American foreign policymaking during the Reagan years. They also offered valuable insights into how we might meet the national security challenges of tomorrow. And it is with that in mind that we have published them in this collection.

We want to thank Peter Schweizer for his outstanding work in assembling and editing this collection. We are also pleased to acknowledge the organizers of the symposium: Charles Palm, deputy director of the Hoover Institution, and Rinelda Bliss, chief of staff at the Center for Security Policy. Without their contributions, the event would not have been nearly as successful as it was. Preparation of this volume took place with the very able assistance of Pat Baker, executive editor of the Hoover Press.

We call to your attention two other related Hoover volumes: *Collapse of Communism* (Hoover Press, 1999), a collection of scholarly essays, edited by Lee Edwards, analyzing communism in the twentieth century; and *CNN's Cold War Documentary: Issues and Controversy* (Hoover Press, 1999), a collection of critical articles, edited by Arnold Beichman, assessing CNN's Cold War documentary television program and book, which generated significant controversy among some historians of the Cold War period.

John Raisian	Roger W. Robinson Jr.
Director	*Chair*
Hoover Institution	*William J. Casey Institute of*
Stanford University	*the Center for Security Policy*

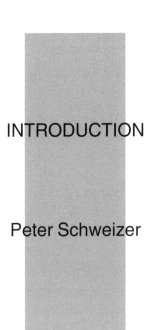

INTRODUCTION

Peter Schweizer

ON MONDAY, February 22, 1999, a symposium was convened at the Willard Inter-Continental Hotel in Washington to examine in detail the policies and people assembled by President Reagan that materially contributed to the end of the Cold War.

Before an audience of over 300 former Reagan administration officials and other policy-practitioners—including former Cabinet officers and senior military officers, scholars, industry leaders, and members of the press—several of the key architects of Reagan foreign policy offered insights into the roots of a strategy that worked to undermine Soviet power. Among the participants were: the Honorable Richard V. Allen, who served as Candidate Reagan's chief foreign policy adviser and went on to serve as President Reagan's first National Security Adviser; the Honorable William P. Clark, President Reagan's second National Security Adviser, former Deputy Secretary of State, and former Secretary of the Interior; the Honorable Edwin Meese III, former Counselor to the President and Attorney General under President Reagan; Dr. Fred Iklé, Under Secre-

tary of Defense for Policy during the Reagan administration;
Frank F. Gaffney Jr., President of the Center for Security Policy
and former Acting Assistant Secretary of Defense during the
Reagan administration; and the Honorable Roger W. Robinson
Jr., former Senior Director of International Economic Affairs
in the Reagan National Security Council.

The symposium was preceded by an elegant luncheon at
which the family of the late William J. Casey presented Mr.
Casey's papers to the Hoover Institution Archives. The luncheon featured introductory remarks by Herbert Hoover III,
Chairman of the Board of Overseers at the Hoover Institution,
Mr. Meese, and Mr. Casey's daughter, Bernadette Casey
Smith. Following a moving tribute to her father, Mrs. Smith
was joined by her mother, Mrs. Sophia Casey, in formally turning over Mr. Casey's personal papers to the Hoover archives.

The Casey papers constitute a particularly rich collection,
documenting half a century of key events in American history.
The collection will become a permanent part of the Hoover
Institution Archives.

Following the luncheon, panelists convened to discuss
what role Reagan administration policies may have played in
the collapse of the Soviet Union. Discussion was based on an
introductory essay written by Hoover Fellow Peter Schweizer
(reprinted below). The event was moderated by Roger Robinson, formerly with the Reagan National Security Council and
the current holder of the William J. Casey Institute's William
J. Casey Chair. Robinson outlined the symposium's objectives, notably to "dispel the myths seemingly intended to di-
minish President Reagan's principled, moral leadership as well
as that of those who served with him in the trenches of the
Cold War."

Peter Schweizer then summarized his essay, describing the
Reagan plan for denying Moscow Western life support and

stressing its fragile economy. Schweizer noted that although the conventional view in the West during the early 1980s held that the Soviet economy was quite healthy, senior Reagan administration officials as well as the president held a decidedly different view. This led to a belief that exploiting Soviet economic vulnerabilities would provide a strategic advantage in the superpower competition.

Exploiting these vulnerabilities took several forms, including heightening the "burdens of empire" by compelling Moscow to spend more of its critical resources to remain viable in the military competition and to support its allies around the globe. It also included efforts to reduce Soviet hard-currency earnings in the West. In both of these respects, Schweizer argued, Reagan administration Cold War policies represented a dramatic break from the past.

Hoover Senior Fellow Richard V. Allen then took the podium and examined the ideas and personal history of Ronald Reagan that shaped his Soviet policy. Drawing upon his experience as Candidate Reagan's chief foreign policy adviser and as his first National Security Adviser, he noted that Ronald Reagan had several experiences that contributed to his moral and political views concerning communism.

In addition to an early experience with communism in the 1940s Hollywood labor union movement, Reagan had other encounters that shaped his views. During his first visit to the Berlin Wall, Allen noted, the future president's "countenance darkened, and he stood before it in silence for several minutes before turning to [us] saying, 'We have got to find a way to knock this thing down.'" He had a similar reaction when he ventured into East Berlin and witnessed common citizens being harassed by the state police.

Allen also noted that Reagan did not accept a status quo view toward the Soviet Union, but instead was a voice within the Republican Party in the 1960s and 1970s condemning the "intellectual and moral bankruptcy of U.S. policy toward the Soviet Union." To ensure that his approach would be different, Candidate Reagan went about recruiting advisers, often with the help of Richard Allen. As Allen noted, "Better than anyone, Ronald Reagan knew that policy does not exist as an abstract notion. To implement it, the right people are indispensable. . . ."

One of those campaign advisers was Dr. Fred C. Iklé. After Richard Allen described the foundational aspects of Reagan's views toward communism in general and the Soviet Union in particular, Dr. Iklé took the podium to describe some of the policies that were implemented to undermine Soviet power. Currently a Distinguished Scholar at the Center for Strategic and International Studies, Iklé focused on two key features of the strategy in which he was intimately involved in shaping: the Reagan defense buildup and export controls.

Iklé began by building on what Richard Allen had said earlier: namely, that Reagan policies were profoundly different from those of his predecessors because of his view toward the Soviet Union. In particular, he noted that the Reagan administration "never accepted the notion that we ought to *stabilize* the Soviet Union." The administration believed that what kept the Cold War going was not a "simple misunderstanding," noted Iklé, but the nature of the Soviet system itself. The administration's conclusion was that bringing the Cold War to an end required changing the Soviet system.

According to Iklé, in the military sphere that meant blunting the Soviet buildup and compelling them to attempt to compete in a way they could not. U.S. defense spending grew from $134 billion in the last Carter year to $282 billion in the seventh Reagan year, more than doubling.

There were also changes in arms policy. In the early 1980s,

Europe was the site for a serious policy dispute over intermediate nuclear forces (INF). The Soviet Union had already started deploying a large number of missiles. The Carter administration had sought to cope with this threat by preparing for the deployment of countervailing missiles but also negotiating with Moscow for an arms control solution. Much of Europe wanted to move ahead on negotiations and hold back on the deployments.

At the Pentagon, Richard Perle, who was Iklé's deputy, came up with the so-called zero-zero solution. The goal in diplomacy would not be reductions in INF, but their elimination. It was a profound break from U.S. policy and presented Moscow with a conundrum, according to Iklé.

President Reagan wrought changes in the strategic field as well. Rejecting the policy of mutual assured destruction (MAD), he moved forward with the Strategic Defense Initiative (SDI), which profoundly worried the Kremlin.

President Reagan's National Security Adviser when SDI was launched spoke next. Discussing his role for the first time publicly since he had left that office sixteen years earlier, William P. Clark outlined how Reagan's strategy vis-à-vis the Soviet Union was put into place. Clark was responsible for supervising the creation and implementation of the key National Security Decision Directives (NSDDs) that shaped the Reagan Soviet strategy.

Clark described in great detail how one very important document, NSDD-75, was crafted, and how that policy statement radically shaped U.S. Soviet policy. Clark noted that whereas it had always been the objective of the U.S. policy toward the Soviet Union to combine containment with negotiations, NSDD-75 added a third objective—namely, encouraging antitotalitarian changes within the USSR and refraining from assisting the Soviet regime to consolidate further its hold on the country. "The basic premise behind this approach," said Clark, "was that it made little sense to seek to stop Soviet imperialism externally while helping to strengthen the regime internally."

To obtain that objective, NSDD-75 identified "a combination of economic and ideological instrumentalities." The United States began efforts to avoid subsidizing the Soviet economy or unduly easing the burden of Soviet resource allocation decisions. In the ideological competition, noted Clark, "the United States would strongly affirm the superiority of Western values, expose the double standards employed by the Soviet Union in dealing with difficulties within its own domain and the outside world, and prevent the Soviet Union from seizing the semantic high ground in the battle of ideas."

Clark then discussed the question of revisionism. He noted that President Reagan's favorite admonition was, "You can accomplish anything if you don't worry about who gets the credit." Clark ended by saying, "If he [Reagan] were here to comment on what is going on in academia today, he would tell us, again, not to worry about it."

Clark concluded by saying that although Reagan had a profoundly moral component to his anticommunist views, this had less to do with anticommunism than his profound belief in the "dignity of human life." He noted that the well known "evil empire" speech "was not so much about the Soviet Union as it was about Ronald Reagan." It was not simply a rejection of communism but an affirmation of human life.

One of the men closest to Reagan is Edwin Meese III, who served as Counselor to the President, a member of the National Security Council, and later as Attorney General. After Clark concluded his remarks, Meese took the podium to outline the other aspects of the Reagan strategy, including the

Reagan Doctrine in the developing world and efforts to invigorate intelligence operations.

Meese began by discussing the difficult situation that President Reagan faced when he took office on the 21st of January 1981. "We had an underfunded military . . . in terms of foreign policy we had an acquiescence to virtual, perpetual, coexistence with the Soviet Union and an acceptance of the inevitable continuance, if not triumph, of socialism as an economic doctrine. . . ."

According to Meese, there was also an even more bleak situation as it related to the status of U.S. intelligence. During the 1970s, he noted, intelligence sources and methods were seriously damaged by the Church Committee in Congress and by the dismissal of more than 700 key agents from the CIA during the latter years of the Carter administration. These disruptions made it difficult for policymakers to have solid information with which to make wise decisions. Therefore, according to Meese, reinvigorated intelligence became a priority for the newly sworn-in President Reagan.

For that job he picked William J. Casey, who had served as the head of secret intelligence in Europe during the Second World War and was a key figure in the successes of the Office of Strategic Services (OSS). Casey was appointed Director of Central Intelligence and set about not only revitalizing the intelligence community in terms of greater funding and recruitment, but also in terms of its analytical work. Casey implemented a strong policy of competitive analysis, in which the president and other key decisionmakers were given analysis from a variety of people looking at the same situation but often with conflicting views.

Meese went on to describe three other areas in which he believes Reagan policies contributed to the demise of the Soviet Union. He echoed what William Clark had said concerning "engaging the Soviet Union on a moral level." He noted that Reagan not only comdemned communism, but spoke of the superiority of Western values. He was an optimist who believed that not only communism was "evil," but the West could triumph if it demonstrated enough willpower. A second important element in the Reagan success was halting Soviet aggression. He noted that during his term in office, "there was not one square kilometer of new soil that fell beneath the boots of Soviet troops."

Meese noted that a third element might have been even more critical—and that was Reagan's "determination to roll back the prior aggression through support of Freedom Fighters around the world, and particularly in the developing world."

During the 1970s, the Soviet Union had rapidly expanded its influence in the developing world. The number of Warsaw Pact and Cuban troops in the Third World had increased some 500 percent over the course of that decade. Furthermore, they had expanded their reach to a number of countries near the strategic choke points of the West, including the Panama Canal, the Straits of Gibraltar, the Suez Canal, the Straits of Hormuz, and the sea lanes of East Asia.

Countries such as Afghanistan, Angola, and Cambodia were kept under Marxist control by more than 300,000 Soviet, Cuban, and Vietnamese troops. Half a dozen other countries— Ethiopia, Nicaragua, South Yemen, Cuba, and Vietnam—were controlled by committed Marxist-Leninist governments with military assistance from the Soviet bloc.

The Reagan administration worked hard to reverse that tide. Much of the work was done by CIA director William J. Casey, who oversaw support for Freedom Fighters in Nicaragua and Afghanistan. Meese cited two examples to outline some of the successes the administration had in the developing world. "The Red Army was defeated in Afghanistan. And in Central America, El Salvador is safe from communist domination and Nicaragua is now a democracy rather than a second bastion of Marxism in our own hemisphere."

Meese concluded his remarks by looking at present-day U.S. foreign policy. He noted that "our national security apparatus is in the hands of many of the people who contributed to the problems in the 1970s that Ronald Reagan had to correct in the 1980s." Meese cited military shortcomings as a particular area of concern, saying "our military situation is in great jeopardy." National defense is being undermined in three ways: lack of funding and budgetary support for our armed forces; a deployment policy and operating tempos that are straining the armed forces by constantly stretching the military; and a policy of "social engineering" in which the Clinton administration is experimenting on our men and women in uniform by implementing a variety of damaging policies, including changing the traditional policies relating to homosexuals in the armed forces.

The present state of world affairs was very much on the mind of Frank Gaffney, who addressed the audience on the topic "Where Do We Go From Here?" Gaffney, President of the Center for Security Policy who formerly served as the Acting Assistant Secretary of Defense during the Reagan administration, tried to apply the lessons of the Reagan foreign policy success to the present security challenges that we face.

Gaffney argued that several fundamental principles underlay the Reagan approach: peace through strength, commitment to individual freedom and economic opportunity, and steady, competent U.S. leadership in international affairs.

Gaffney issued a call to arms for those who continue to believe that these principles should guide U.S. foreign policy. He urged citizens to hold their elected leaders accountable on important national security matters, noting that with the spread of technology new threats emerge quickly and next time the challenge we face "will be a come-as-you-are party" in which we won't "have the opportunity to prepare ourselves."

He urged that greater attention be focused on what he called "the nexus between U.S. national security and international economic, financial, and technology developments," an approach that was used during the Reagan years. "This is a trend that Bill Casey foresaw and addressed with extraordinary, if all too characteristic, acumen."

Gaffney also urged that efforts continue to be made to teach the history of the Reagan years. "It is not enough for those of us who had the privilege of being part of it to remember and to share anecdotally some of our insights. It must be conveyed to future generations." He noted that the Cold War "may be the first war in history whose story is being written by the losers—the intellectual elite that embraced moral equivalence if not the Soviet cause itself."

Finally, he urged that the United States "implement at long last Ronald Reagan's single most important national security initiative," the deployment of an effective antimilitary system capable of ending America's current vulnerability to attack.

1

The Fall of the Berlin Wall after Ten Years

AN ESSAY

Peter Schweizer

A DECADE AGO the most visible symbol of the Soviet empire was destroyed as the Berlin Wall was broken into rubble. The image of thousands of German citizens standing on the wall with chisels and hammers in hand, striking a blow against the large, gray, once imposing structure, is still one of the most enduring images of our time.

The dissolution of the Soviet Empire was a central event of the twentieth century—but it is also one of the most puzzling. To borrow from the poet T. S. Eliot, the end of the Soviet system "came not with a bang but a whimper." Soviet communism was not the victim of a noisy civil war, which has befallen other empires throughout history. Nor did the end result from an orderly, planned retreat from power, as with the British Empire after the Second World War. Rather, the Soviet edifice simply collapsed under its own weight.

For decades, perhaps centuries, historians will debate

which factors weighed most on the Soviet system. Was it the bankruptcy of the Marxist-Leninist ideology? Was Soviet failure preordained because communism proved so contrary to human nature? Did the calcified and rusting Soviet economy finally bear such a burden that it imploded, much like a weak roof collapsing under the burden of heavy snow?

The answer, in short, is all of these explanations and many more. Yet there is the curious but critically important question of timing. Why did the collapse occur precisely when it did? This question is of fundamental importance when assessing causes. Ideological failures, systemic crises, and economic catastrophes in Soviet history were nothing new and had been present from the beginning. They were in a real sense fundamental to the system. Marxism-Leninism had been discredited in the eyes of the public and even in the hearts of many Communist Party members well before 1980. Likewise, economic failure was a constant in Soviet life. As the growing collection of materials in Russian Archives Research Projects at the Hoover Institution makes clear, economic trauma was a problem for Moscow dating back to the 1920s.[1] Given these constants, something changed in the 1980s that pushed Soviet communism over the brink.

One factor that deserves serious exploration is the external pressures that were brought to bear on the system. During the 1980s, the United States adopted a series of policies designed to burden and undermine the Soviet system. The Reagan administration was clearly the most anticommunist administration of the Cold War era. Far from representing a continuation of the policy of containment that had guided U.S. post-war

---

1. See Gordon M. Hahn, "An Autopsy of the Soviet Economy: Soviet Documents Now in the Hoover Archives Reveal Seventy Years of Economic Bungling," *Hoover Digest*, No. 4, 1998, pp. 174–77.

Soviet policy since Truman, Reagan administration policies represented a profound change in dealing with Moscow. Were these policies the critical ingredient that pushed the Soviet Union to collapse?

Despite a large library of books on the end of the Cold War, there has been scant investigation of the role U.S. policy might have played in hastening the collapse of the Soviet Union. Rather, the focus of study has been almost exclusively on the policies of Soviet General Secretary Mikhail Gorbachev. This lack of interest as to whether the United States hastened the demise of the Soviet Union is particularly unusual given the long-standing belief among scholars and policymakers that U.S. policy could influence and affect domestic developments in Russia.

Since the earliest days of the Cold War, both hawks and doves largely embraced the notion that the West could influence the course of events in the Soviet Union. The only real debate was over how best to achieve such influence. Hawks tended to argue, for example, that Moscow's behavior could be modified through military deterrence. This provided the basis for U.S. military policy throughout the Cold War period. Doves, on the other hand, held that Moscow could be influenced by diplomacy and accommodation. Détente was an effort to use both approaches. Henry Kissinger, usually a hawk on military affairs, argued that the West could "moderate" Soviet conduct through economic contact. "In a crisis," he wrote as Secretary of State, "we thought that the fear of losing markets and access to raw materials, Western technological innovations or bank credits, would produce Soviet caution."[2]

This belief that Washington could influence events in Moscow was not confined to U.S. policymakers and scholars.

---

2. Quoted in *New Republic*, February 17, 1982, p. 14.

Russian observers shared the view that the United States could directly influence internal events in their country. Soviet dissident Andrei Sakharov, the most outstanding dissident figure of the Cold War era, said human rights improvements in Russia were possible only as a result of Western influence.[3]

One would be hard pressed to find many observers during the Cold War who argued that the United States had *no* influence on events in the Soviet Union. In the post–Cold War era, however, this has essentially become the model for studying the end of the Cold War. The demise of the Soviet system resulted from internal events exclusively, the argument goes. To the extent that Reagan administration policies are discussed in the context of the ending of the Cold War, they are described as a impediment to the process of reducing tensions.[4]

This approach is not only intellectually inconsistent and dubious, but it also makes for poor history. Examining the demise of the Soviet Union in isolation from U.S. policies during the crucial years just prior to the collapse is somewhat akin to studying the collapse of the Confederacy at the end of the American Civil War by studying Jefferson Davis and Robert E. Lee without looking at the strategies employed by Abraham Lincoln and Ulysses S. Grant. Although certainly not the sole cause of the Soviet demise, the policies adopted by the Reagan administration nonetheless played an important role in the drama.

3. *New York Times Magazine,* June 8, 1980, p. 110.
4. See, for example, Raymond Garthoff, *The Great Transition: American-Soviet Relations and the End of the Cold War* (Washington: Brookings Institution, 1994).

COURAGE AMIDST BLEAKNESS

In retrospect it is difficult to put into perspective how out of tune with established opinion the early Reagan administration was in its views toward the Soviet Union. Early on President Reagan declared that the Soviet Union was "an evil empire" that "could not be trusted." He went on to call the Kremlin a "brutal and thuggish regime." In these heady post–Cold War days it is easy to assume that this moral tone and the call for hard-line anti-Soviet policies were widely accepted.

Today there is a general consensus that Soviet communism represented a bleak period for human history. Russian President Boris Yeltsin made this moral assessment fashionable in a June 1992 speech to the U.S. Congress. "The world can sigh in relief," he declared. "The idol of communism which spread everywhere social strife, animosity, and unalleled brutality, which instilled fear in humanity, has collapsed." Yeltsin was implicitly aligning himself with Reagan's view of the Soviet Union as an "evil empire" and he received thunderous applause from everyone in the chamber.

In the early 1980s, however, such views were hardly welcome in leading Western circles. The United States and the West had witnessed a rapid expansion of Soviet power during the previous decade, and the Kremlin had made serious advances around the globe. In Vietnam, along China's southern border and astride the sea lanes that brought Persian Gulf oil to Japan, they had a new ally. By occupying Afghanistan, Soviet forces came 500 miles closer to the warm-water ports of the Indian Ocean and to the Strait of Hormuz through which came the oil essential to Western Europe. In the Horn of Africa, new allies dominated the southern approaches to the Red Sea and the southern tip of the Arabian peninsula. In southern

Africa, proxies held the sources of minerals the industrial nations required. Moscow even had allies in the Caribbean and Central America, on the very doorstep of the United States.

During the 1970s the West granted Moscow cherished political objectives. Détente provided the Soviets with de facto recognition by the West of their imperial holdings in Central Europe. Various treaties that the Brandt government in West Germany concluded with the Soviet Union, the Helsinki Declaration of 1975, and the deliberations of the Conference for Security and Cooperation in Europe gave them the political legitimacy they had long yearned for.[5]

In the shadows of the Vietnam War, U.S. leaders had been openly reassessing the merits of anticommunism. President Jimmy Carter, in a 1977 speech to Notre Dame University, blamed the Indochina imbroglio on "our inordinate fear of communism." He went on to argue that the U.S. defeat in Southeast Asia was therapeutic for the nation. "Through failure we have found our way to our own values," he declared.

These views reflected established opinion throughout the West, which saw U.S. power on the wane and communist authority as legitimate. The *New York Times* greeted victory for Pol Pot in Cambodia with the headline "For Most, a Better Life." When it became apparent in 1980 that martial law might be declared in Poland, German Chancellor Helmut Schmidt said such a move was "necessary" to stabilize the country. Some U.S. officials even went so far as to openly and publicly question the ethics of using the nuclear deterrent in the face of Soviet aggression. Former Defense Secretary Robert McNamara, for one, repeatedly declared his view that the U.S.

---

5. For more on this subject, see Eugen Loebl, "Moral Values and U.S. Foreign Policy: An End to the Age of Hypocrisy?" *Strategic Review*, Spring 1986, pp. 27–35.

nuclear deterrent was an illusion because no president in his right mind would dream of using it to counter a Soviet attack. "In long private conversations with successive presidents— Kennedy and Johnson," he revealed, "I recommended, without qualification, that they never initiate, under any circumstances, the use of nuclear weapons. I believe they accepted my recommendations." This statement constituted an admission that the centerpiece of NATO's whole strategy had been a bluff since its inception.[6]

Public opinion, if less accepting of communist legitimacy, was nonetheless tepid in the face of the Soviet challenge. In 1982, for example, polls indicated that 70 percent of the U.S. population believed that a freeze of nuclear weapons was the best means for dealing with the Soviet military threat—even if such a deal guaranteed Soviet strategic superiority.[7] Public opinion in Western Europe was hardly more encouraging. In a 1981 survey, 40 percent of West Germans unconditionally opposed the stationing of U.S. missiles on their soil, regardless of how many missiles the Soviet Union deployed and targeted on Germany. Nearly the same proportion rejected resorting to nuclear weapons ever, even in retaliation for Soviet nuclear strikes.[8]

Given the temper of the time, Russian novelist and Nobel Laureate Aleksandr Solzhenitsyn was left to declare in 1980 that the West seemed "exhausted" in the face of the Soviet threat, lacking the moral strength to challenge the legitimacy of Soviet power. "No weapons, no matter how powerful, can

---

6. "The Military Role of Nuclear Weapons: Perceptions and Misperceptions," *Foreign Affairs*, Fall 1983, p. 79.

7. Fox Butterfield, "Anatomy of a Protest," *New York Times*, July 11, 1982.

8. U.S. International Communication Agency, Office of Research, Briefing Paper, B-12-23-81.

help the West until it overcomes its loss of willpower. In a state of psychological weakness, weapons become a burden for the capitulating side."[9]

The psychological climate of the time reflected more than a waning commitment to anticommunism. Many leading Western intellectuals, while not embracing the tenets of Marxism-Leninism, concluded that the Soviet system worked and could meet the basic needs of the populace. Indeed, Soviet communism was often described as a legitimate alternative to the free market economies of the West. In 1977, for example, Pierre Mauroy, soon to be France's prime minister and later first secretary of the Socialist Party, wrote in a book called *Inheritors of the Future*, "In 1975 I went to the Soviet Union and in Kharkov, Kiev, and elsewhere I always found the same vitality. In elementary schools, in high schools, I found the faith and the enthusiasm which had characterized the schools of the Third Republic. They had made astounding economic gains; their victories in the field of technology are victories for all the people. . . ." This from a man who was in charge of France between 1981 and 1984.

Attitudes among intellectuals and leaders in the United States were hardly much better. The distinguished historian Arthur Schlesinger Jr. declared after a 1982 trip to Moscow that the Soviet system worked quite well. "I found more goods in the shops, more food in the markets, more cars in the street—more of almost everything, except, for some reason, caviar." Noted economist John Kenneth Galbraith lauded the Soviet system in 1984 as in some respects superior to the liberal economies of the West. "The Russian system succeeds because, in contrast to the Western industrial economies, it

9. Aleksandr Solzhenitsyn, "The Exhausted West," in *Détente* (New Brunswick, N.J.: Transaction Books, 1980).

makes full use of its manpower," he claimed. "The Soviet economy has made great national progress in recent years." Professor Lester Thurow at the Massachusetts Institute of Technology (MIT) said in his textbook *The Economic Problem* that the Soviet economy was comparable to our economic machine. "Can economic command significantly compress and accelerate the growth process? The remarkable performance of the Soviet Union suggests that it can. In 1920, Russia was but a minor figure in the economic councils of the world. Today it is a country whose economic achievements bear comparison with those of the United States."

Distinguished Sovietologist Seweryn Bialer of Columbia University argued in *Foreign Affairs* that the Soviet system was stable because of how well it functioned. "The Soviet Union is not now nor will it be during the next decade in the throes of a true systemic crisis for it boasts enormous unused reserves of political and social stability that suffice to endure the deepest difficulties." Nobel Laureate Paul Samuelson put it even more strongly in his textbook *Economics* (1981) when he challenged the assumption that communism couldn't work: "It is a vulgar mistake to think that most people in Eastern Europe are miserable."

It was into this intellectual and political malaise that Ronald Reagan stepped in 1981. However, far from embracing this prevailing orthodoxy, the president and his closest advisers rejected it. The administration boldly and openly challenged the moral basis of communism and the view that accommodation with Moscow was a necessary fact of life. To the astonishment and consternation of leading intellectuals, the president and members of his administration made no bones about the fact that they saw the Soviet Union as the eventual loser in the Cold War. "The years ahead will be great ones for our country, for the cause of freedom and the spread of civilization," the president told students at Notre Dame University in May 1981, barely four years after President Carter had delivered his conciliatory speech at the same location. "The West will not contain communism, it will transcend communism. We will not bother to denounce it, we'll dismiss it as a sad, bizarre chapter in human history whose last pages are even now being written."

In June 1982, Reagan's message to the British Parliament was very much the same. "In an ironic sense, Karl Marx was right," he said. "We are witnessing today a great revolutionary crisis—a crisis where the demands of the economic order are colliding directly with those of the political order. But the crisis is happening not in the free, non-Marxist West, but in the home of Marxism-Leninism, the Soviet Union. . . . . What we see here is a political structure that no longer corresponds to its economic base, a society where production forces are hampered by political ones." The president declared that Marxism-Leninism would be left on the "ash heap of history" and predicted that Eastern Europe and the Soviet Union itself would experience "repeated explosions against repression." On March 8, 1983, in his famous "evil empire" speech, Reagan again proclaimed, "I believe that communism is another sad, bizarre chapter in human history whose last pages even now are being written."

Members of the president's inner circle also publicly rejected the conventional view of the Soviet Union. On May 9, 1981, CIA director William J. Casey, in a speech to the Business Council, described the Soviet economy as "showing increasing weakness." A "growing internal discontent," he said, was gripping the country. On June 16, 1982, Thomas Reed, a consultant to the National Security Council and special assistant to the president, declared in the *New York Times* that the Soviet Union was "an economic basket case," and the United

States "should not provide the trade and credits necessary to prop up the Soviet economy."[10]

History reveals that the assessment made by President Reagan and many of his advisers proved to be far more accurate than those of our leading intellectual lights. But it is easy to forget the ridicule and personal attacks that the president and his advisers were subject to for their views. Shortly after President Reagan gave his "evil empire" speech, for example, Strobe Talbott in *Time* magazine noted his agreement with "other administration officials, especially professional diplomats and intelligence analysts with long experience in Soviet affairs [who] . . . expressed confidence that the Soviets recognized such theorizing for what it was: idiosyncratic, extremist, and very much confined to the fringes of government."[11] Anthony Lewis of the *New York Times* called these statements "terribly dangerous," and "outrageous." He went on to lecture the president on his need to learn that "in the real world . . . there is no escape from the hard work of relating to the Soviet Union."[12]

Historian Arthur Schlesinger Jr. joined the chorus of scorn, ridiculing the administration while contending "those in the U.S. who think the Soviet Union is on the verge of economic and social collapse, ready with one small push to go over the brink, are . . . only kidding themselves." He compared those in the administration who espoused such views with the crusty old guard in the Kremlin who saw capitalism in its final stages. Both sides were "wishful thinkers," he said, who "always see

10. "Soviet Economy Called 'Basket Case,'" *Washington Post*, June 17, 1982.

11. Strobe Talbott, *The Russians and Reagan* (New York: Random House, Vintage, 1984), p. 75.

12. Anthony Lewis, "What Reagan Wrought," *New York Times*, June 21, 1984.

other societies as far more fragile than they are. Each super-power has economic troubles; neither is on the ropes." Mark Hertsgaard, like many others, cited remarks by the president on the failures of communism as proof that he was a "simple-minded ideologue" and a "reckless cowboy."[13]

Speaker of the House Tip O'Neill even went so far as to question the president's mental faculties for expressing such views. In the Speaker's meetings with high-ranking Soviet officials, he warned Soviet Ambassador Dobrynin that "Reagan will give vent to his primitive instincts . . . probably put us on the verge of a major armed conflict. He is a dangerous man."[14]

THE STRATEGY

From the vantage point of Moscow, Reagan was indeed a "dangerous man," though not because he sought war with the Soviet Union. The new administration represented a threat because it intended to act on its convictions. President Reagan believed that Soviet communism was evil and vulnerable. As Anatoly Dobrynin put it in his memoirs, the president's anti-communism was "not just some political pose." From its earliest days, the Reagan administration adopted a coherent policy designed to roll back Soviet power in a manner and form never seen before. Soviet officials were certainly aware of what the administration was doing. Soviet Foreign Minister Andrei Gromyko complained to former U.S. Senator George McGovern in 1984 that Reagan and his aides "want to cause trouble. They want to weaken the Soviet system. They want to bring

13. Mark Hertsgaard, *On Bended Knee: The Press and the Reagan Presidency* (New York: Farrar Straus and Giroux, 1988), p. 134.

14. See Anatoly Dobrynin, *In Confidence: Moscow's Ambassador to America's Six Cold War Presidents* (New York: Times Books, 1995).

it down." He told President Reagan the same thing in the Oval Office.[15]

The Reagan approach to the Soviet Union represented a stark break with the past. Since 1947, Soviet policy in Washington had been based on containment, defined as an effort "to block further expansion of Soviet power."[16] From that policy grew a web of treaty alliances with nations around the world, military assistance to threatened allies, and in some cases direct U.S. military intervention. By the 1970s, a stripped-down version of containment known as détente emerged, adding a litany of inducements in the hope of inviting a change in Soviet conduct.

Containment, however, was by design a defensive strategy, forcing the U.S. to simply react to Soviet probes. It was a policy designed to maintain the status quo, accepting Moscow's domination of Central Europe and control of satellite states around the world.

The Reagan strategy was fundamentally different in that it was a mix of both defense and offense. The strategy called for deterring Soviet aggression, but also exploiting Soviet weaknesses in the hope of rolling back communist power. The approach was specifically laid out in a now-declassified National Security Decision Directive (NSDD) signed by President Reagan. NSDD-75 called for rolling back communist power around the world and undermining the Soviet economy. The document did not say that the U.S. would confront the Soviets at every point, but rather that the U.S. would look for vulnerabilities and try to exploit them.

Identifying specific vulnerabilities and determining how

---

15. Don Oberdorfer, *The Turn* (New York: Poseidon, 1991), p. 89.

16. For a solid history of containment, see John Lewis Gaddis, *Strategies of Containment* (New York: Oxford University Press, 1982).

best to exploit them required detailed intelligence. Tradition-
ally, the Central Intelligence Agency (CIA) had tracked Soviet
military developments, political intrigues, and broad economic trends. CIA director William J. Casey, to meet the demands of the new strategy, rapidly broadened the agency's
study of the Soviet threat far beyond these traditional areas.
Casey established the CIA's Center for the Study of Insurgency
and Instability, which tracked Soviet efforts in the developing
world and sought to identify economic and political fissures
that could be exploited. The CIA also established the Technology Transfer Center, to track Soviet efforts to acquire Western
technology. In the analysis division, Casey launched a program to conduct "vulnerability assessments" of the Soviet
Union. Early on, for example, he discovered that Moscow's
economic situation was more desperate than anyone imag-
ined. In 1980 Moscow had sold 90 tons of gold on world markets; but in 1981, the Kremlin had dumped 240 tons in a very
soft world market. It was the first time such a detailed analysis
of Soviet economic, political, and military "weak points" had
been done. For all of his work in this area, the Kremlin singled
out the CIA director for particular criticism, describing him in
one TASS commentary as a "Queens [New York] gangster."

Through the CIA vulnerability assessments and further
analysis by the National Security Council (NSC) under Richard Allen and William Clark, two core weak points were identified. A portrait emerged of the Soviet bloc as an empire with
political and ethnic ruptures that substantially weakened its
power. Nationalism, religious ferment, and ethnic conflict
caused flashpoints around the Soviet world in places such as
Poland, Afghanistan, and Nicaragua. Indigenous forces in
those countries and elsewhere were eager to challenge Soviet-
backed regimes and could prove to be potent allies.

The other critical weak point was the Soviet economy. The

Reagan administration recognized early that the Soviet economy was slowing and progressively less able to meet the increased demands made on it by expanding military and imperial commitments. The Kremlin was a military superpower but an economic dwarf. Moscow could produce advanced military systems, but had trouble keeping civilian factories running properly. The superpower relied on inputs from the West—high-technology exports, bank credits, and hard currency from energy exports to stay afloat. Constricting those critical inputs would significantly hamstring the Soviet economy.

THE REAGAN DOCTRINE

Undermining Soviet geopolitical power meant supporting indigenous forces inside the Soviet bloc in their struggle against communist rule—in other words, trading places in the "national liberation" struggle. For decades, Moscow had backed insurgents operating against U.S. allies in the developing world, Southeast Asia, Africa, and Central America. By the early 1980s, however, there were opportunities for the United States to reverse course and do the same to the Kremlin. President Reagan argued that as a matter of principle, the United States should always encourage those fighting against Soviet-backed governments and, when possible, back them with material support. Eventually this policy became known as the "Reagan Doctrine," a low-risk, low-cost policy to roll back Soviet power.

This approach to the Third World was a remarkable change from the past. Under Nixon, for example, the United States showed little concern for the Third World as a matter of strategic choice or priority. The Nixon administration was preoccupied with the Vietnam War and took strong action in the

Indo-Pakistan and the Yom Kippur wars. It did try to achieve a better calibration of U.S. policy and interests through the Nixon Doctrine, which meant providing aid to allies in the developing world who were fighting insurgencies; but there was no strategic approach to the developing world.

Under Carter, the United States became obsessed with gaining acceptance in the developing world and failed to understand the strategic dimensions of the superpower competition in those regions of the globe. There was a sentimentalism about the Third World, personified in the appointment of Andrew Young as ambassador to the United Nations. Carter failed to respond strongly to Soviet gains in the Horn of Africa. Although the Carter administration offered support to the mujahedeen fighting Soviet occupation in Afghanistan, they never saw that conflict as an opportunity to roll back Soviet power.

When U.S. forces pulled out of Vietnam, the United States was left without an intellectual structure with which to approach the Third World.[17] The Reagan administration created one, arguing that the United States would challenge existing Soviet assets in the developing world at points of our choosing. The Reagan Doctrine showed that it was possible to have your cake and eat it: The administration could crusade for human rights while also enhancing our national power and interest.

U.S. military assistance and intelligence support flowed to anticommunist forces in Afghanistan, Nicaragua, Cambodia, and Angola. Nonmilitary assistance and diplomatic help were given to the Solidarity movement in Poland. By the middle of the decade, the Soviets were clearly put on the defensive. Whereas in the 1960s and 1970s they spoke the language of

17. For a greater discussion, see Charles Krauthammer, "Regaining the Initiative," *National Interest*, Summer 1988, pp. 145–47.

national liberation, Gorbachev at the 1987 Washington summit spoke of "the need to respect the wishes of people to determine their own future." The eventual success of the policy was striking. President Reagan entered the White House after a Marxist-Leninist revolution had just been established in Central America. He left the White House shortly after Moscow admitted defeat on its own border in Afghanistan. Even in instances where anticommunist forces did not ultimately win on the battlefield, the cost was still high for Moscow. The Soviet bloc had to pump more than $1 billion per year into Nicaragua in 1986 and 1987.

Much of the actual implementation of the Reagan Doctrine fell to CIA director William J. Casey. For him, the Reagan Doctrine was a passion that grew out of his experiences in the Second World War. Casey had served as a young Navy lieutenant in the Office of Strategic Services and his job included running covert operations behind Hitler's lines. In his book *The Secret War Against Hitler* (a posthumously published chronicle of his wartime experiences), he clearly drew the connection between the use of insurgents against Hitler and their usefulness against contemporary tyrants. "I believe that it is important today to understand how clandestine intelligence, covert action, and organized resistance saved blood and treasure in defeating Hitler," he wrote. "These capabilities may be more important than missiles and satellites in meeting crises yet to come, and point to the potential for dissident action against the control centers and lines of communication of a totalitarian power."[18]

In the end, the Reagan Doctrine offered startling results in

---

18. William J. Casey, *The Secret War Against Hitler* (Washington: Regnery, 1988), p. xiv.

two countries at distant points on the globe, Afghanistan and Poland.

AFGHANISTAN

In many respects the most important flashpoint in the developing world during the 1980s was Afghanistan. While the civil war in Nicaragua received much of the national news attention during the 1980s, it was in Afghanistan that the Reagan Doctrine was most completely implemented and Soviet prestige put directly on the line. Moscow's defeat in this mountainous country profoundly shook the Kremlin's confidence.

The human cost of Soviet occupation in Afghanistan was staggering. In terms of population, no nation occupied by Hitler's Germany experienced the suffering that Afghanistan underwent in the first six years of Soviet rule. Over one million Afghans were killed, and four million others had to flee the country.

When Soviet forces had stormed across the Afghan border in 1979, the response from the West was largely muted. French and German leaders were at first inclined to look the other way and write off the invasion. India, though a democracy, cynically approved of the Soviet move. In the United States, the Carter administration imposed a grain embargo and offered low-level military aid to the indigenous Afghan forces (mujahedeen) who were fighting Moscow. But the intelligence finding signed by the president authorizing assistance said the U.S. objective was simply to "harass" Soviet forces.

Under the Reagan administration, Afghanistan became an opportunity to roll back Soviet power and as a result efforts to support the mujahedeen rapidly expanded. In 1981, the mujahedeen received 10,000 tons of arms and ammunition from the

United States. By 1985, the level of support rose to 65,000 tons and cost more than $100 million per year. The administration also actively solicited financial support for the mujahedeen from other countries, including Saudi Arabia, Kuwait, and Bahrain. The cost to Kremlin coffers was an estimated $3 to $4 billion per year.

However, 1985 proved to be the critical year in the war, one that laid the foundation for the Kremlin's first outright military defeat of the Cold War. In March, President Reagan signed top-secret NSDD-166, which articulated for the first time specific objectives with regard to the Afghan war and put them in a strategic context. Whereas the aim under President Carter had been to "harass" Soviet forces, the goal according to NSDD-166 became outright military victory.

To achieve that end President Reagan made several key decisions. He authorized, at Bill Casey's request, extending the war into the Soviet Union itself. The suggestion had originally arisen in the White House in a 1983 Oval Office meeting of President Reagan, National Security Adviser Bill Clark, and Casey. But only after the Pakistani Intelligence Service (ISI), which was managing the flow of CIA aid to the Afghans, and mujahedeen commanders embraced the idea, was it adopted.

In 1986, specially trained units working inside the Soviet Union, equipped with Chinese rocket launchers and high-tech explosives provided by the CIA, sought out Soviet military targets for sabotage. They hit Soviet industrial sites, derailed trains, and fired rockets at Soviet military installations. By the end of the year, reports of mujahedeen activity inside the Soviet Union were substantial. Muj commanders in the northern provinces of Afghanistan were issued 107-mm Chinese rocket launchers and 122-mm Egyptian rocket launchers with ranges of almost ten miles. By night the systems were set up on the southern bank of the Amu River to fire volleys onto Soviet territory. Teams specially trained by the ISI and equipped by the CIA made their way across the Amu to hit Soviet border posts, lay mines, and knock down power lines. An airfield just north of the Soviet town of Pyandzh was repeatedly hit by muj commandos.[19]

Coinciding with these attacks, the CIA also began supplying the mujahedeen with sophisticated Stinger antiaircraft missiles. By the middle of 1986, the muj began bringing down twenty to forty Soviet planes and helicopters per month. The Soviets had counted on total mastery of the air to win; Stinger missiles destroyed this key advantage. "The use of Stingers tipped the tactical balance in our favor," recalls Mohammad Yousaf, who directed the CIA covert supply operation to the muj for Pakistani intelligence. "As success followed success, so the mujahedeen morale rose and that of the enemy fell."[20] The introduction of the Stinger to the battlefield imposed a trauma on the Soviet psyche that cannot be overestimated. Sergei Tarasenko, principal foreign policy assistant to Eduard Shevardnadze, recalls, "I went with Shevardnadze to Afghanistan six times . . . and when we were coming into Kabul airport, believe me, we were mindful of Stinger missiles. That's an unpleasant feeling. You were happy when you were crossing the border and the loudspeaker would say, 'We are now in Soviet territory. Oh, my God. We made it!'"[21]

The Soviet defeat in Afghanistan was a direct result of the

19. Perhaps the best detailed account of the conduct of the Afghan war is Brigadier Mohammad Yousaf and Mark Adkin, *The Bear Trap: Afghanistan's Untold Story* (London: Leo Cooper, 1992). Yousaf directed the covert supply program as a senior official in the Pakistan Intelligence Service.

20. See Yousaf and Adkin, *Bear Trap*.

21. Sergei Tarasenko, quoted in William C. Wohlforth, ed., *Witnesses to the End of the Cold War* (Baltimore: Johns Hopkins University Press, 1996), p. 141.

Reagan policies. Absent a coherent strategy to win in Afghanistan, ballooning military support, and Stinger missiles, Soviet forces might have remained in Afghanistan. As it was, in November 1986, less than a year after these policy changes took effect, a decisive meeting took place in Moscow in which the Soviet Politburo made its fateful decision to pull out of Afghanistan.[22] Retreat meant reduced Soviet ability to project power to South and Southwest Asia. Defeat also contributed to weakening the system. It contained the seeds for the destruction of a range of Soviet ideological and doctrinal positions—commitment to other communist revolutions, to the idea of the "march of history," and to the Brezhnev Doctrine. Retreat also raised doubts about Soviet resolve in Eastern Europe and communist Third World countries, leading to greater instability there. Just as the military defeats in 1905 and 1917 had revolutionary consequences for Tsarist Russia, defeat in Afghanistan lead to profound changes in Soviet Russia.

POLAND

Afghanistan was a bloody shooting war where the Reagan Doctrine played a central role, but the battle for freedom in Poland was a twilight struggle where indigenous forces used printing presses and protests to fight the Soviet-backed regime. Reagan administration efforts to roll back Soviet power also played a critical role in the triumph of freedom in the heart of Europe, however.

In late 1981 Poland seemed to be slowly sliding out of the Soviet orbit. Thousands of activists were in the streets on a regular basis and the Solidarity movement, with the tacit support of the Catholic church, was openly questioning the legit-

22. See Oberdorfer, *The Turn*, pp. 239–43.

imacy of communist rule. Poland was the geopolitical linch-
pin of Soviet rule in central Europe and the most important
non-Soviet member of the Warsaw Pact. In December 1981
Polish military authorities, with the encouragement of Moscow, declared martial law. Under the guise of the Orwellian
sounding Operation Springtime, the regime arrested opposition leaders and shut down organizations that were not party-
sanctioned.

The response from the Reagan administration was direct
and swift. As with Afghanistan, the administration saw Poland as an opportunity to eventually roll back Soviet power. In
early 1982, in response to martial law, President Reagan signed
NSDD-32, which outlined a multipronged strategy to weaken
Soviet influence and strengthen indigenous forces in central
Europe. NSDD-32 made clear that the United States would
covertly support underground movements in the region who
were attempting to throw off communist rule; intensify psychological operations directed at the region, particularly radio
broadcasts such as Voice of America and Radio Free Europe;
and seek through diplomacy and trade to wean the regimes
from their reliance on Moscow.

Consequently, only a few months after martial law was
declared, the United States began providing covert assistance
to the Solidarity underground. Funds were used to buy computers and printing presses for underground activists, communications equipment for the Solidarity leadership, and even
funds for opposition radio stations. At its peak by the middle
of the decade, this support amounted to approximately $8 mil-
lion per year.[23]

23. For details of this covert financial support, see Carl Bernstein, "The
Holy Alliance," *Time*, February 24, 1992; and Peter Schweizer, *Victory: The*

Even more importantly, the Reagan administration linked trade and financial ties between the United States and Poland with the survival of Solidarity. The administration didn't simply express concern about general human rights conditions in Poland; instead, it was keenly interested in the fate of Solidarity as a vital alternative to the Polish regime.

When the Polish government outlawed Solidarity, the Reagan administration suspended Poland's most-favored-nation (MFN) trading status with the United States. Suspending MFN increased tariffs on Polish products exported to the United States by 300 to 400 percent and effectively priced them out of the U.S. market. In the four years following the proclamation of martial law, the Polish government tried to crush the Solidarity movement by arresting the leadership, harassing members, and shutting down opposition printing presses. All the while, covert U.S. support flowed to the movement and U.S. sanctions were taking a large economic bite. A cataclysmic economic decline began to unfold. In 1980, trade with the West had amounted to $7.5 billion. By 1986 it had dwindled to a paltry $1 billion. As a result, bank loans from the West also declined. Unable to export to the West, Poland could not get credit. Before 1980, Warsaw had been able to borrow up to $8 billion annually; by 1985, loans were down to $300 million.

Eventually, the failure to crush Solidarity and the accompanying economic bite from U.S. sanctions forced the Polish government to make peace with Solidarity. On July 22, 1986, Warsaw declared a general amnesty and all political prisoners were freed. The enemies of the regime were returned to the streets, free to rejoin the opposition. At the request of Solidar-

Reagan Administration's Secret Strategy That Hastened the Collapse of the Soviet Union (New York: Atlantic Monthly Press, 1994).

ity, U.S. sanctions came to an end, but covert funding to the Polish opposition continued.

Fearing a renewal of sanctions, the Polish government never again attempted to destroy Solidarity. When national elections were held in 1989, the path was paved for freedom. For Moscow, those elections signaled the beginning of the end. According to Sergei Tarasenko, principal foreign policy assistant to Foreign Minister Eduard Shevardnadze between 1985 and 1991, elections convinced Mikhail Gorbachev that the Soviet system would break up.[24] However, absent a coherent U.S. policy designed to roll back Soviet power, the triumph of freedom might not have occurred. It is highly unlikely that Solidarity would have even survived the decade and forced elections without the overt and covert support of the Reagan administration.

ECONOMIC WARFARE

Parallel to pushing Soviet power back geographically, the Reagan administration sought to undermine the shaky Soviet economy. In one of the few public pronouncements on the subject at the time, National Security Adviser Bill Clark summarized the principles of a 1982 National Security Decision Memorandum on the subject this way: "We must force our principal adversary, the Soviet Union, to bear the brunt of its economic shortcomings."[25] Relying on the vulnerability assessments produced by both the CIA and the NSC, the admin-

24. Sergei Tarasenko, quoted in Wohlforth, *Witnesses to the End of the Cold War*, pp. 112–13.

25. "Reagan Aide Tells of New Strategy on Soviet Threat," *New York Times*, May 22, 1982.

istration identified specific economic sectors that could be hurt.

Through the Reagan Doctrine, the Kremlin was already being forced to expend billions to hold on to their imperial assets. The Reagan administration also saw the arms competition between the two superpowers as a means by which the Kremlin could be compelled to spend even more precious resources.

DEFENSE SPENDING AND STRATEGIC DEFENSE

One of President Reagan's earliest priorities when he took office in 1981 was to restore the strength of what he saw as a dangerously weak military deterrent. Consequently, the administration undertook the largest peacetime buildup in U.S history. The Pentagon budget rose by 13 percent in 1981 alone. Procurement budgets increased by nearly 25 percent per year and the overall budget doubled between 1980 and 1985. By the middle of the decade, U.S. military expenditures exceeded those of the Soviet Union for the first time since the late 1960s.

In the first six years of the Reagan presidency, the Pentagon purchased nearly 3,000 combat aircraft, 3,700 strategic missiles, and about 10,000 tanks, a procurement rate roughly double that of the 1970s. Most importantly, perhaps, these new systems were more sophisticated than ever. Spending on research and development doubled during Reagan's first term.[26]

There was more to this buildup than restoring U.S. military capability. The Reagan administration understood economic realities in the Soviet Union. As the Soviet economy was not growing very much, the military sector could increase

---

26. Caspar Weinberger, Annual Report to the Congress, FY 1986.

only at the expense of consumption and investment in the
civilian sector. Moscow was competing with the West militar-
ily by using an increasing share of the economy for military
purposes.

In early 1982, the Pentagon put together a top-secret, five-
year planning directive laying out administration objectives
for the budget. Crafted under the guidance of Defense Secretary Caspar Weinberger, the directive offers important insights
into precisely how the Reagan administration planned to use
the military competition between the superpowers to undermine the Soviet economy. Along with restoring U.S. capabilities, the document made clear that the buildup was part of an
"economic and technical war" against Moscow. The *New
York Times* noted "as a peacetime complement to military
strategy, the guidance document asserts that the United States
and its allies should, in effect, declare economic and technological war on the Soviet Union."[27]

The Reagan defense buildup was a form of economic and
technical war because it placed great emphasis on developing
advanced high-tech weapons systems. The five-year planning
directive set as a goal: "Investment in weapon systems that
render the accumulative Soviet equipment obsolete." As Soviet General Makhmut Akhmetovich Gareev put it, under
Reagan the U.S. defense buildup was "sharply intensifying . . .
at a pace and in forms never noted before."[28]

New U.S. weapons systems were being developed and deployed which did indeed threaten Soviet systems with obsolescence. Soviet General K. U. Kardashevskiy conducted a series

27. Richard Halloran, "Pentagon Draws Up First Strategy for Fighting a
Long Nuclear War," *New York Times*, May 30, 1982.

28. Makhmut Akhmetovich Gareev, *M. V. Frunze: Military Theorist* (Mc-
Lean, Va.: Pergamon-Brassey's, 1988), p. 395.

of technical studies in the early part of the decade and con-cluded that the Kremlin's armor units—the backbone of their conventional forces—might be threatened with obsolescence by the growing arsenal of high-tech and advanced U.S. anti-tank systems. Another Soviet analyst lamented, "The West prefers to invest funds in improvements of antitank weapons, thus creating a need for us to constantly modernize our tank fleet and as a result pushing us toward ever greater expenditure of economic resources."[29]

In his 1982 book *Always on Guard in Defense of the Fatherland*, Soviet Marshal Nikolai Ogarkov likewise expressed a deep concern about the "fast pace" of U.S. technological de-velopment. He warned, "In these conditions, the failure to change views in time, and stagnation in the development and deployment of new kinds of military construction, are fraught with serious consequences."

Soviet officials saw the Reagan defense buildup as a threat to their military capability and standing in the world. "Over-all, viewed from Moscow, the U.S.–Soviet military balance seemed to be tilting in favor of the United States—and along with it, the perceived aggregate 'correlation of forces,'" recalls Sergei Fedorenko, a division chief with the USA and Canada Institute of the Soviet Academy of Sciences.[30]

Former Soviet Foreign Minister Aleksandr Bessmertnykh remembers the same. "The thrust of the reports that were coming to the political leadership was that after a certain pe-

---

29. Vitaly Shlykov, "The Armor Is Strong," *Mezhdunarodnaya Zhizn*, November 1988. See also Peter Schweizer, "The Soviet Military Today: Go-ing High-Tech," *Orbis: A Journal of World Affairs*, Vol. 35, no. 2, pp. 195–206.

30. Sergei Fedorenko, "Roots and Origins of the Protracted Soviet Crisis," in *The Soviet Union After Perestroika: Change and Continuity* (Washington: Brassey's, 1991), p. 87.

riod of accommodations [détente of the 1970s] the United
States had suddenly with a new president who came to Washington, President Reagan, decided to change the course of defense policy and start an enormous buildup. All the leaks and
the all the reports that we were getting from our own intelligence in the United States . . . indicated that the United States
was serious about overwhelming the Soviet Union in one basic
strategic effort."[31]

The high-tech military challenge to Moscow became even
more pronounced in early 1983 when President Reagan revealed his plans to research and eventually develop a strategic
defense system.[32] In a March 23 address to the nation, President Reagan outlined his commitment to a new direction in
the strategic field. Rejecting the doctrine of Mutual Assured
Destruction (MAD), he announced that the United States
would begin research on the Strategic Defense Initiative (SDI).
"Let me just say I am totally committed to this course," he
said, concluding his remarks. Two days later, the president
issued an executive order in which he instructed National Security Adviser William Clark to supervise an "intense effort"
to define a long-term research and development program for
the system.

President Reagan was totally committed to making a strategic defense system work, but he also understood that even if
the system were never deployed, the program could still prove
useful if it compelled Moscow to spend precious resources to
meet the challenge. The presidential directive authorizing SDI

31. Aleksandr Bessmertnykh, quoted in Wohlforth, *Witnesses to the End
of the Cold War*, p. 31.
32. For a discussion of how U.S. military technologies have influenced
Soviet resource priorities from the atomic bomb to strategic defense, see
Matthew Evangelista, *Innovation and the Arms Race* (Ithaca, N.Y.: Cornell
University Press, 1988), pp. 218–67.

specifically mentioned that its success would be measured in part by a "cost-effective criterion," including the economic burdens it imposed on Moscow.

Throughout his two terms in office, President Reagan remained steadfastly committed to the project. Funding more than doubled from FY 1985 to almost $3.3 billion in FY 1987. The administration was also working to bring other advanced nations into the program. The Pentagon signed a series of SDI collaboration agreements with major Western allies, including Britain (December 1985), Germany (March 1986), Israel (May 1986), Italy (September 1986), and Japan (July 1987), adding substantial scientific and technical abilities to the research program. The Strategic Defense Initiative grew quickly from an idea to an international research program Moscow felt it had to match. By late 1986, the SDI project was beginning to show some notable technical successes.

SDI hit the Soviets at their point of greatest vulnerability in the military competition—high technology. According to a Department of Defense assessment, Moscow was ten years behind the United States in computer electronics and trailed in many of the most important revolutionary technologies—electro-optic sensors, robotics and machine intelligence, signal processing, stealth, and telecommunications.[33] For this reason, the SDI program created real concern in Moscow. "I remember these days pretty well," recalls former Soviet Foreign Minister Aleksandr Bessmertnykh. "The atmosphere in Moscow was very tense for the first few years of the Reagan

33. Department of Defense, FY 1986 Department of Defense Program for Research, Development, and Acquisition (Washington: U.S. Government Printing Office, 1986), pp. 11–15.

administration, especially because of the SDI system: It frightened us very much."[34]

Although many Western scientists remained skeptical
about the ability of strategic defense to work, Moscow acted
as if success were a given. Oleg Gordievsky, a KGB officer in
London and a double agent for British intelligence, provided
reports to his handlers of the Soviet military's assessment.
Colonel A. I. Sazhin, a military attaché at the Soviet embassy
in London, told a group of diplomats and intelligence officers
that the armed forces believed the SDI system might prove 90
percent effective, according to Gordievsky. Sazhin added he
saw little chance of the Soviets' being able to keep pace with
the United States.[35]

The KGB view was similar. A February 1985 KGB report
Gordievsky provided to Western intelligence reveals that the
Kremlin believed the Reagan administration was "striving to
gain military superiority over the Soviet Union." The Strategic
Defense Initiative was "widely publicized as an effective
method of defense of the whole population of America in a
nuclear war," the report noted. The report went on to say there
was the possibility that the United States was hoping "to draw
the USSR into a costly arms race in an area where according to
American estimates it is lagging behind the USA."[36] Publicly,
Kremlin leaders expressed their view that the SDI program
was a serious threat. As the leading government newspaper
Izvestiya put it: "They [the Reagan administration] want to
impose on us an even more ruinous arms race. They calculate

34. Aleksandr Bessmertnykh, quoted in Wohlforth, *Witnesses to the End
of the Cold War*, p. 14.

35. Christopher Andrew and Oleg Gordievsky, *Instructions from the Centre: Top Secret Files on KGB Foreign Operations* (London: Hodder and Stough-
ton, 1991), p. 107.

36. Ibid., pp. 112–13.

that the Soviet Union will not last the race. It lacks the resources, it lacks the technical potential. They hope that our country's economy will be exhausted."[37]

As a result of the U.S. high-technology military buildup, massive resources flowed into Soviet military programs. The Soviet defense budget was set to rise 45 percent between 1981 and 1985, but by late 1983 Soviet officials deemed this increase insufficient to match the Reagan buildup. In the spring of 1984 General Secretary Konstantin Chernenko announced that "the complex international situation has forced us to divert a great deal of resources to strengthening the security of our country."[38] The diversion entailed committing even more resources to the high-tech military sector. According to Roald Z. Sagdeev, who headed the Soviet Space Research Institute in the 1980s, Moscow spent tens of billions of dollars responding to SDI . "This program became priority No. 1 after Mr. Reagan's announcement of the 'Star Wars' in 1983." These were funds the Kremlin could ill afford to spend. Sagdeev believes this expenditure of resources weakened the Soviet Union and may have contributed to its demise.[39]

The Reagan military buildup did more than further burden the Soviet economy: It also forced the Kremlin to bring about structural change and reform. After the death of General Secretary Konstantin Chernenko, a Soviet soft-liner emerged in the midst of the U.S. military challenge. According to the traditional model of studying the Soviet Union, the opposite should have happened. The traditional view was that the Kremlin leadership responded to the West with a tit for tat, meeting belligerence with belligerence and accommodation

37. "Chances Missed, Search Continues," *Izvestiya*, October 17, 1986.
38. *Krasnaya Zvezda*, March 3, 1984.
39. *New York Times*, August 18, 1993, pp. A1, A15.

with accommodation. But in 1984 the Politburo chose, in response to Reagan's anticommunism, a man committed to perestroika and disarmament.

In a very real sense, the Reagan defense buildup was the
impetus for perestroika and the rise of Gorbachev. As early as
1981, the Soviet Ministry of Defense had produced a monograph noting the necessity of countering the U.S. high-tech
buildup and the need to reform the economy in order to effectively compete. Entitled *The Economic Basis of the Defense
Might of a Socialist State*, it noted that the continued decay of
the Soviet high-tech industrial sector "could decelerate the
development of the very basis of military power—the economy—and therefore inflict irreparable damage on the defense
capability." With the Reagan defense buildup, the rules of the
superpower military competition were changing, forcing Moscow to master high technology. Doing so was of fundamental
importance to Soviet security interests. As Soviet Foreign
Minister Eduard Shevardnadze described the new reality, "It
is not so much a state's stock of weapons which are of decisive
significance for its security as the ability to create and produce
fundamentally new weapons."[40]

Gorbachev also saw Moscow's ability to compete as resting on mastery of high-technology. Failure to effectively compete with the United States meant declining Soviet power.
"Without an acceleration of the country's economic and social
development," he warned, "it will be impossible to maintain
our positions on the international scene."[41]

Moscow was indeed falling behind—and trying to keep up
threatened to exhaust the Soviet system. "The United States
wants to exhaust the Soviet Union economically through a

---

40. Eduard Shevardnadze, quoted in *Mezhunardnaya Zhizn*, no. 11, 1988.
41. Quoted in Oberdorfer, *The Turn*, p. 162.

race in the most up-to-date and expensive space weapons," Gorbachev told people on Moscow television. "It wants to create various kinds of difficulties for the Soviet leadership, to wreck its plans, including the social sphere, in the sphere of improving the standard of living of our people, thus arousing dissatisfaction among the people with their leadership."[42] According to Aleksandr Bessmertnykh, this fear of having to compete with the United States became "the number-one preoccupation of Gorbachev. When we were talking about SDI, just the feeling that if we get involved in this SDI arms race, trying to do something like the United States was going to do, to do space programs, space-based weapons, et cetera, looked like a horror to Gorbachev."[43]

To relieve the pressure, Gorbachev attempted to convince President Reagan, at the 1986 Rejkavik Summit, to abandon SDI in favor of deep cuts in nuclear weapons. President Reagan refused, remaining steadfastly committed to the program. As a result, Gorbachev increasingly found himself devoting more resources than ever to defense. The Soviet five-year plan announced in 1986 called for more spending on advanced weapons. As Gorbachev would later admit, the planned rate of growth for defense in 1986 through 1990 was almost 8 percent per year, twice the rate of national income growth. All told, defense expenditures rose an astonishing 45 percent over that five-year period. By the middle of the decade, the best Soviet resources in the field were being directed toward the military-industrial base. Half of the machine tools were going to defense enterprises, which also employed the best scientists. At least half of all research and development expenditures were

42. Mikhail Gorbachev, Soviet television, October 14, 1986.
43. Aleksandr Bessmertnykh, quoted in Wohlforth, *Witnesses to the End of the Cold War*, pp. 47–48.

for the armed forces.[44] Consequently, fewer resources were available for the civilian economy.

STEMMING THE FLOW OF TECHNOLOGY

Raising the costs for the Kremlin through the Reagan Doctrine and the defense buildup was only half of the administration's strategy. As Moscow was forced to spend more precious resources, the United States also sought opportunities to reduce Kremlin access to critical Western inputs that allowed the Soviet economy to limp along. Western bank loans, imported technology, and energy exports were all identified as key resources that provided lifeblood to the Soviet economy. Stemming the flow of technology was an early priority.

For decades the Soviet Military Industrial Commission had engaged in a massive effort to acquire Western technology. By the early 1980s, an estimated 100,000 people were working in the USSR just translating foreign technical documents. Imported technologies were applied to both civilian military projects with great effect.

A steady flow of intelligence on Soviet high-technology espionage began to appear in the spring of 1981 that indicated just how profitable stealing and acquiring technology could be. The French counterintelligence service (DST) had a source in the KGB code-named FAREWELL, who was in the scientific and technical branch of the intelligence service's elite First Chief Directorate.[45] Over the course of the late 1970s, FAREWELL passed along more than 4,000 documents on how the

---

44. Mikhail Gorbachev, "Speech to Nizhniy Tagil Workers," Moscow Domestic Television Services in Russian, 1545 GMT, April 27, 1990.
45. For more details on the FAREWELL case, see Nigel West, *Games of Intelligence* (New York: Crown, 1989).

KGB was seeking specific technologies in the West, how Soviet "companies" and the Soviet Military Industrial Commission were set up, and how agents were dispatched abroad to buy and steal embargoed scientific material.

The documents also revealed how Moscow reaped a bountiful harvest from these efforts. The papers revealed that from 1976 to 1980, for example, the Ministry of the Aviation Industry alone saved $800 million in research and development costs through the illegal acquisition of Western technology. That alone represented over 100,000 man-years of scientific research. The Soviets were also obtaining 100 million computer circuits a year, purchasing manufacturing cells, and even complete production lines from the West. By the late 1970s, Moscow was diverting billions of dollars' worth of high-tech items from Western Europe, Asia, and the United States every year.

As a result, restricting Soviet access to Western high technology became an early Reagan administration priority. NSDD-66, a presidential directive written by NSC staff member Roger Robinson, described where the damage could best be done. Robinson identified a "strategic trade triad" of three critical resources from the West that Moscow relied upon to sustain its economy: high-technology imports, bank credits, and hard currency from energy exports.

The administration feverishly worked to reduce Soviet access to Western technology. In October 1981, at the behest of the administration, the U.S. Customs Service began Operation Exodus, a program to disrupt sales of U.S. technology to Moscow. During the 1970s, only two or three technology theft cases were prosecuted by the federal government. Operation Exodus called for aggressive enforcement of export laws. The rise in prosecutions was dramatic. By January 1986, the U.S. Department of Justice was prosecuting more than one hundred cases per month. The administration also worked to limit the number of high-technology goods that could be legally shipped to the Soviet bloc by expanding the Commodity Control List. Twenty-six technology items were added to the list between October 1983 and September 1987. By 1986, about 40 percent of all U.S. manufacturers' exports required an export control license of some sort, making the legal export of advanced U.S. technologies to Moscow extremely difficult.

Soviet access to Western technology was an international problem, however. Many U.S. allies had exported openly to the Soviets during the era of détente. So the Reagan administration aggressively pushed for broad restrictions on exports from allied countries. Much of the success in this area was the result of strenuous diplomacy.

The U.S. Export Act of 1979 gave the president the option of restricting access to U.S. technology to foreign countries or companies that did not cooperate on export issues. The Reagan administration used the act to pressure three neutral countries—Sweden, Switzerland, and Austria—to limit their role as a transshipment point for high-tech materials going to Moscow. The effort made use of both the carrot and the stick. In Sweden, for example, companies such as L. M. Ericsson AB and ASEA AB were threatened with reduced access to the U.S. market when accused of high-technology exports to the Soviet bloc. On the other hand, if Swedish companies and officials cooperated with Washington, U.S. export licenses would treat Swedish companies as generously as allied countries, a very lucrative privilege.

In 1985 the Export Administration Act of 1979 was amended. The amendments gave U.S. export enforcement officials the power for the first time to investigate illegal exports outside the United States. Agents could track down technology exports in locales such as Hong Kong, Switzerland, and

India. Bilateral agreements signed with several neutral foreign countries led these countries to police their own exports. Customs officials also received other additional powers. They could now search suspicious shipments without warrants and could seize suspect shipments. The penalties for illegally shipping goods also became much more stringent: prison sentences instead of fines.

The Coordinating Committee for Multilateral Export Controls (COCOM), which included all NATO countries (save Iceland) and Japan, also tightened the noose on technology. In July 1984 COCOM completed a review of the international embargo list on technology exports to the Soviet bloc. At the urging of the Reagan administration the three lists of restricted technologies—munitions, atomic energy, and international—were revised and expanded. Added were computer software, telecommunications equipment, and small military-relevant computers. The parameters of enforcement were tightened, particularly in the area of halting the transshipment of goods through third countries. Members of COCOM agreed to coordinate efforts to halt illegal shipments.

Monitoring the flow of technology to the Soviet bloc largely fell to the CIA. Director William J. Casey established a Technology Transfer Committee at Langley to track Soviet-bloc technology acquisitions. It served as a clearinghouse to which twenty-two departments in the federal government contributed manpower and other resources. Pressure from Casey led several major Western allies to set up similar entities, albeit on a smaller scale. In 1984 the British Ministry of Defense created a technology transfer unit staffed by technical specialists to monitor high-tech exports. Similar projects were launched in Paris and Bonn.

Within the first few years of the administration the results of these efforts became apparent: There was a dramatic decline in high-technology exports to the Soviet Union. In 1975, of all the manufactured goods sold to the Soviet Union by the United States, 32.7 percent were high-tech products. That amounted to $219 million in sales. By 1983, high-tech sales represented only 5.4 percent, amounting to a paltry $39 million.[46] Exports by U.S. allies declined as well. Members of CO-COM acted on over one hundred U.S. recommendations regarding exports to the Soviet bloc in 1981 and 82 alone. Better policing began to have a significant effect. By the fall of 1983, U.S. Customs investigators, in collaboration with their European counterparts, had been able to seize approximately 1,400 illegal shipments valued at almost $200 million. Many of these were critical technologies that Moscow hoped would help sustain Soviet industry.[47] Little wonder that Soviet officials complained bitterly about these efforts. As Radomir Bogdanov, deputy director of the USA and Canada Institute and a former senior official with the KGB, told Don Oberdorfer of the *Washington Post*: "You [Americans] are trying to destroy our economy, to interfere with our trade, to overwhelm and make us inferior in the strategic field."[48]

The constriction of high-technology exports to the Soviet Union led to shifting priorities for the KGB, which became increasingly desperate to find effective means to acquire advanced Western technology. In the "Work Plan for 1984," Vladimir Kryuchkov, head of the KGB's First Service, told his agents: "Taking into account the additional measures adopted by the adversary, in the first place the USA, to reinforce control over observance of secrecy and the embargo on export of

46. U.S. Department of Commerce, International Trade Administration, "Quantification of Western Exports of High-Technology Products to Communist Countries Through 1983 (Washington, 1985), pp. 12, 28, 29.
47. "Geheimclub COCOM," *Die Zeit*, October 10, 1983, p. 34.
48. Oberdorfer, *The Turn*, p. 76.

commodities, scientific and technical intelligence, we must analyze the existing situation in greater depth and discover fresh resources for dealing with scientific and technological intelligence."[49]

How much did these efforts by the Reagan administration damage the Soviet economy? It is impossible to calculate the complete cost, but studies indicate that it was likely to be on the magnitude of billions of dollars per year. A formal report entitled "Total Effect of Technology Transfer on U.S./Western Security, a Defense Department Overview," informally called the Aggregate Assessment, was issued by the Pentagon in December 1984. A team of engineers examined seventy-nine technology export licenses that had been denied over the past year and tried to determine the value the exports would have had to the Soviet industrial base. The estimated price tag for these technologies alone was between $500 million and $1 billion per year for twelve years in additional research and development costs and manpower. The government was denying thousands of exports per year, so the total cost to Moscow was undoubtedly much higher.[50]

ENERGY EXPORTS TO THE WEST

High technology was not the only important input from the West that was deemed vital to the Soviet economy. If technology imports helped overcome critical inefficiencies in the Soviet economic machine, hard currency from energy exports to the West provided badly needed funds. NSDD-66 identified

---

49. KGB report no. 2126/PR, November 11, 1983, in Andrew and Gordievsky, *Instructions from the Centre*, pp. 16–33.

50. "U.S. Tallies Cost to Soviets of Technology Transfer Rules," *Aviation Week and Space Technology*, December 14, 1984, p. 67.

energy exports as another key component of the "strategic
trade triad." As the directive pointed out, Moscow's ability to
export oil and natural gas to the West greatly aided their efforts
to sustain the struggling economy. Vulnerability assessments
conducted by the CIA concluded that oil and natural gas exports made up between 60 and 80 percent of Soviet hard currency earnings during most years.

Critical in determining the level of Soviet hard currency
income was the price of world energy. During the decade of
the 1970s when the price of oil had gone through the ceiling,
Moscow's hard currency earnings from oil went up 272 percent, even though the volume of exports increased only 22
percent. The CIA estimated that for every one dollar increase
in the price of a barrel of oil, Moscow would gain nearly $1
billion in hard currency. But the converse was also true. A drop
in the price of oil by perhaps $10 a barrel would cost Moscow
nearly $10 billion.

In the late 1970s and early 1980s the largest and most critical economic venture for the Soviets was known as Urengoi
6. It was slated to be the most substantial deal in East-West
trade history. The project was a natural gas pipeline running
3,600 miles from Northern Siberia's Urengoi gas field to the
Soviet-Czech border, where it would be attached to a Western
European gas grid that would dispense 1.37 trillion cubic feet
of gas a year to a French, Italian, and West German consor-
tium. It was designed to be a two-strand line, providing Moscow with as much as $30 billion per year in hard currency from
sales. To a country with annual hard currency earnings of
about $32 billion a year, it represented an enormous financial
boon.

The Carter administration failed to express much concern
about the project when it was announced, but from the earliest
days of the Reagan administration, cabinet members such as

Bill Casey and Caspar Weinberger expressed deep reservations about the project. It was rightly seen as a cash cow for Moscow, which would make Western Europe dangerously dependent on Soviet energy. Casey, Weinberger, and some members of the NSC throughout 1981 openly called for an embargo of U.S. gas and oil equipment that was necessary to complete the project. The U.S. Office of Technology Assessment declared that such a move would be "tantamount to economic warfare," which is precisely what it was intended to be. Others, particularly the State Department, opposed an embargo. The debate over the pipeline ensued until martial law was declared in Poland in December 1981. With that move, the debate was settled. President Reagan, eager to punish Moscow for the crackdown, announced an embargo on December 29.

The embargo effectively halted two massive Soviet energy projects. The Urengoi natural gas pipeline project required advanced U.S.-designed rotor shafts and blades driving the turbines for the forty-one compressor stations along the 3,300-mile line. The embargo also halted Japanese and Soviet plans to develop oil and gas fields off Sakhalin Island. The Japanese deal required sophisticated drilling technologies from General Electric, Dresser Industries, Schlumberger, and Velco to make it work. The Sakhalin Island project was also at a critical stage. Plans were to begin drilling in the spring, and the Kremlin had been counting on several billion dollars a year in income from this project, which called for exploiting proven reserves of 1.1 billion barrels of oil and 2.5 billion cubic feet of gas.

In Western Europe, however, U.S. allies were firmly against sanctions. Indeed, France, Germany, and Britain spoke openly about circumventing the embargo. European licensees had access to the U.S. technologies needed for the projects, so British Prime Minister Margaret Thatcher and French President François Mitterrand told their companies to ship equipment for the pipeline in violation of the U.S. order. The United States threatened to halt all imports from any European companies that circumvented the embargo. A transatlantic crisis began to brew.

Eventually the differences were hammered out in the fall of 1982. The United States allowed the pipeline project to proceed, but only if the allies agreed to a unified "security-first" allied economic strategy vis-à-vis the Soviet bloc. President Reagan issued a statement summarizing the agreement. "First, each partner has affirmed that no new contracts for the purchase of Soviet natural gas will be signed or approved during the course of our study of alternative Western sources of energy. Second, we and our partners will strengthen existing controls on the transfer of strategic items to the Soviet Union. Third, we will establish, without delay, procedures for monitoring financial relations with the Soviet Union and will work to harmonize our export credit policies."[51]

Although the embargo was lifted, it did produce several important results in the effort to weaken the Soviet economy: The embargo delayed by almost two years both the Sakhalin Island project and the Urengoi pipeline, costing the Kremlin enormous revenue when it was critically needed. The projects were also cut in size as a result of U.S. concerns. At a meeting of the International Energy Agency (IEA) in the spring of 1983, the European allies agreed to cap imports of Soviet natural gas at 30 percent of their energy needs. The agreement was codified at the G-7 Williamsburg Summit in May 1983 and cut the pipeline project in half.

Efforts to reduce Soviet hard currency earnings from energy exports did not end with the flap over the Siberian pipe-

51. See George Shultz, *Turmoil and Triumph* (New York: Scribner's, 1993).

line. In keeping with the vulnerability assessments which had concluded that high oil prices benefited the Soviet economy, bringing world oil prices down was a key objective of the Reagan administration. Such a policy was a win-win for the United States. In early 1983 the Treasury Department completed a massive secret study on international oil pricing which concluded that lower oil prices would be very beneficial to the U.S. economy. The report argued that the optimum oil price for the United States was approximately $20 a barrel, well below the 1983 price of $34. At the time, the United States was spending $183 billion on 5.5 billion barrels of oil a year. Of that, imports amounted to 1.6 billion barrels. The study noted that a drop in international markets to $20 a barrel would lower U.S. energy costs by $71.5 billion per year, transferring income to consumers amounting to 1 percent of existing gross national product. On the other hand, the report noted that dropping oil prices would have a "devastating effect on the Soviet economy." The report noted Moscow's heavy reliance on energy exports for hard currency.

Achieving a drop in oil prices would occur with either a dramatic reduction in demand or a dramatic increase in world production. Concerning the latter, the Commerce Department report mentioned that if Saudi Arabia and other countries "with available oil reserves should step up their production and increase world output by . . . about 2.7 to 5.4 million barrels a day and cause the world price to fall by about 40 percent, the overall effect on the United States would be very beneficial." Saudi Arabia was the only world producer that by itself could rapidly raise production and continue to be profitable with dramatically lower prices. Therefore protecting Saudi Arabia and forging a close relationship became an early and important administration objective.

The Reagan administration, more than any other, worked

to forge trust and cooperation with Riyadh. Only months after coming into office, U.S. Defense Secretary Caspar Weinberger announced that the Rapid Deployment Task Force, proposed by President Carter to protect the oil fields of the Persian Gulf, would be dramatically upgraded and expanded. It became a unified command, with its own forces, intelligence, communications, and its own unified commander, responsible for all aspects of U.S. military planning and operations in the region. The new U.S. Central Command (USCENTCOM), as it was called, would boast nearly 300,000 U.S. troops. (USCENT-COM was the force used by the Bush administration to evict Saddam Hussein from Kuwait.)

The United States also provided sophisticated military weaponry to the Saudis, including AWACS and advanced fighter aircraft and later Stinger antiaircraft missiles. (In May 1984, President Reagan used emergency procedures to bypass Congress and make sure the Stinger sale went through.) In early 1985, the U.S. Air Force broke ground on Peace Shield, the most technologically advanced integrated air defense system outside NATO. Peace Shield is a computerized command, control, and communications system that links Saudi AWACS planes with five underground command centers and seventeen long-range radar stations. It includes a permanent staff of 400 U.S. personnel.

Along with such military support came the hope that the Saudis would push for lower oil prices. "One of the reasons we were selling the Saudis those weapons is because of the hope that lower oil prices would result," former Defense Secretary Caspar Weinberger told me.[52] The United States actively made clear it favored lower world oil prices. In August 1984, Treasury Secretary Donald Regan sent a memo to Energy Secretary

52. Interview with Caspar Weinberger.

Donald Hodel, stating that the United States should push for lower prices by "resisting any pressure on us to prop up oil prices." Shortly thereafter Hodel asked rhetorically in a public speech at an oil conference in London: "Are [oil] customers seeing prices that are low enough?" He didn't answer this question directly, but the implication was that they were not. Several weeks later, Hodel took the highly public and unusual step of sending telexes to major oil companies in the United States criticizing OPEC's efforts "to manipulate the market by setting artificially high prices or by seeking to fashion arbitrary restrictions on production." The administration seemed to be publicly "talking down" oil prices.[53]

There was also a concerted effort at private diplomacy, specifically with Saudi leaders. The message: Lower oil prices were to the benefit of the United States and to the detriment of Moscow and the radical Arab states that threatened Riyadh. CIA Director Bill Casey and Defense Secretary Caspar Weinberger made it clear in private conversations that the United States would favor lower world prices. As Caspar Weinberger put it, "I raised the issue in general discussions with Saudi officials—the defense minister, Prince Bandar, and King Fahd. They knew we wanted as low an oil price as possible. Among the benefits were our domestic economic and political situation, and a lot less money going to the Soviets. It was a win-win situation."[54]

In August 1985, Saudi Arabia did dramatically raise production from less than 2 million barrels to almost 9 million barrels a day. As to be expected, world oil prices plunged. In November 1985, crude oil sold for $30 a barrel; barely five

53. See Edwin S. Rothschild, "The Roots of Bush's Oil Policy," *Texas Observer*, February 14, 1992.
54. Interview with Caspar Weinberger.

months later it stood at $12. Why did the Saudis dramatically raise production? Undoubtedly for a variety of reasons. But the fact that Riyadh felt that it had strong U.S. support amidst regional threats certainly helped them withstand the pressure from radical producers such as Iran and Iraq to keep prices high. Saudi leaders also knew the United States—its chief protector—would support such a move. As Caspar Weinberger put it, "It was an internal Saudi decision to increase production and cause the price of oil to drop in 1985. But it was a decision that they knew would sit very well with the United States."[55]

The oil-price plunge was cataclysmic for Moscow. Almost half of Soviet hard currency earnings evaporated overnight. As a May 1986 CIA report noted, "The sharp drop in world oil prices this year has dramatically altered Moscow's earning position. . . . As in 1985, oil exports to hard currency countries would probably bear the brunt of any production declines. With few short-term opportunities at home for stepping up the pace of energy conservation or oil substitution, reduction in deliveries to domestic consumers probably would disrupt production at a time when Gorbachev is placing a high premium on boosting economic growth." By early 1986, the report noted, it took almost five times more Soviet oil to purchase a given piece of West German machinery than it had a year earlier. The calculated annual loss for Moscow was $13 billion per year.[56]

SHAPING HISTORY

It would be impossible to determine which factor played the most important role in the collapse of the Soviet Union.

---

55. Ibid.
56. "USSR: Facing the Dilemma of Hard Currency Shortages," Central Intelligence Agency: Directorate of Intelligence, May 1986.

Rising nationalism certainly helped to undermine the system, as did the erosion of ideological fervor. What is also clear is that policies adopted and executed by the Reagan administration weighed heavily on the Soviet system. The cumulative effect of these policies was to rob the Soviet economy—annually, by a variety of means—of tens of billions of dollars of critical resources. In addition to the economic toll of these policies, it is clear that they also played a real and direct part in the rolling-back of Soviet power by supporting anticommunist insurgents in Afghanistan and the anticommunist opposition in Poland.

The genius of the Reagan administration approach is not simply the innovative and unique policies that were employed but the courage with which they were pursued. They were politically risky and went against the assumptions that had guided U.S. Soviet policy for decades. The Reagan administration rejected containment for something bolder. Ironically, in this boldness, the administration seemed to be heeding the advice of Karl Marx, who wrote in the December 1853 issue of the *New York Tribune*: "There is only one way to deal with a power like Russia and that is in the fearless way."

How historians will ultimately judge the U.S. role in the demise of the Soviet Union remains to be seen, but those at the center of the drama certainly saw a U.S. hand in these dramatic events. When the Berlin Wall was breached in November 1989 and Germans united in celebration, German Chancellor Helmut Kohl is said to have telephoned the White House to thank the United States. And in 1991, on the day he resigned his office and officially declared the USSR dead, Mikhail Gorbachev took the time to write a long personal letter to Ronald Reagan.

2

Ronald Reagan

AN EXTRAORDINARY MAN
IN EXTRAORDINARY TIMES

Richard V. Allen

THERE IS A WIDESPREAD and an interesting tendency among historians, scribes, and pundits to attribute final victory in the Cold War to factors and causes other than those which actually brought that long, drawn-out struggle to a slow-motion, essentially nonviolent but unmistakable conclusion, beginning in 1989.

One segment of this school, exemplified by the writings of Strobe Talbott, presently Deputy Secretary of State, holds that the administration of Ronald Reagan actually aggravated and prolonged the Cold War through constant provocations and mindless hostility.

As the growing body of literature of recent years shows, however, an increasing number of scholars are reassessing this flawed and simplistic notion. To those of us who had the privilege of participating in the process that eventually led to the end of the Cold War, there are different, more accurate, and demonstrable causes for the ultimate victory, but there is no disagreement whatsoever over details, and they cannot undermine the general agreement that Reagan's leadership was the essential unifying factor.

That leadership did not begin just on January 21, 1981. It has not only important historical roots, but great and important historical momentum that carried well beyond January 20, 1989, when he left office.

EVOLVING VIEWS: THE POSTWAR WORLD

That Ronald Reagan's fundamental attitude toward communists generally and toward the Soviet Union and other communist regimes in particular was shaped by his experience in Hollywood early in the Cold War is undeniable and well documented.

He witnessed the origins of the Cold War, the loss of all of Eastern Europe, the fall of Nationalist China, the Korean War, the Cuban missile crisis, and the beginnings of the war in Vietnam.

His emergence on the national political scene in the 1964 campaign of Barry Goldwater also shaped his beliefs, and by 1968, his first attempt at the presidency, the basic elements of his thinking were cemented into place.

It was in 1976, as he challenged an incumbent president for the Republican nomination, that he began a concentrated focus on developing a comprehensive and coherent national strategy. That campaign was faltering after a series of primary losses, but when he began his spring offensive in 1976, with an attack on the intellectual and moral bankruptcy of U.S. policy toward the Soviet Union, his campaign ignited and he very nearly won the nomination.

"WE WIN AND THEY LOSE:
WHAT DO YOU THINK OF THAT?"

Each of us has very personal memories of how and why we became attracted to the cause that Ronald Reagan so ably and articulately represented, and why we joined in supporting his agenda.

What is striking is that nearly all who joined the effort in the early phases of the Reagan movement came because they were intellectually committed to his views, and not because they might collect fat campaign consulting fees and jobs in a future administration. Equally striking is the fact that the group joined in the Reagan effort was remarkably small, but very efficient.

I would like to relate briefly my own experience. At the Republican Convention in Miami in 1968, then serving as Richard Nixon's foreign policy coordinator, I came upon a small group of men in the lobby of the Fontainebleau Hotel. My friend Phil Crane, then a college professor, pulled me into the crowd to greet Governor Reagan and proceeded to berate me, saying, "Dick, you are on the wrong side here." Eight years and two stints in the Nixon White House later, no longer under the illusion that Richard Nixon was a committed conservative, I knew better. I *was* on the wrong side.

Martin Anderson, my trusted colleague from 1968—and obviously he, too, was on the wrong side in 1968—asked me when he was traveling with Ronald Reagan to write some memoranda during the 1976 campaign, and I did, enthusiastically so. Reagan versus Ford was truly an easy choice.

A few weeks before the Kansas City Convention, the venerable Bryce Harlow called to say that Ford and Reagan forces were at loggerheads over the drafting of the foreign policy portion of the platform and wondered if I, as someone yet uncommitted to either side, would write the draft.

Of course, I was committed, but there was no need to advertise that fact, and I went ahead and did it. That draft, that platform, helped provide the springboard for a surge by Reagan, one that nearly carried him to victory. That platform, an outright repudiation of Nixon-Ford-Kissinger foreign policy, never saw the light of day in the campaign of 1976, just as twenty years later the 1996 platform was buried by the Dole-Kemp campaign, and the candidate remarked that he had not yet bothered to read it.

In January 1977, I visited Ronald Reagan in Los Angeles to ask of him a personal favor relating to my own intentions. He agreed to do the favor, and then he asked if I had some time to talk. During the next four hours, he said many memorable things, but none more significant than this. "My idea of American policy toward the Soviet Union is simple, and some would say simplistic," he said. "It is this: We win and they lose. What do you think of that?"

One had never heard such words from the lips of a major political figure, and until then, we had thought only in terms of managing the relationship with the Soviet Union.

Reagan went right to the heart of the matter. Utilizing American values, strength, and creativity, he believed we could outdistance the Soviets and cause them to withdraw from the Cold War, or perhaps even to collapse. Herein lay the great difference, back in early 1977, between Reagan and every other politician: He literally believed we could win, and was prepared to carry this message to the nation as the intellectual foundation of a presidency.

There was also an obvious danger in such a foreign policy. In the atmosphere of the late 1970s, stating this proposition directly invited frontal attack, even a repetition of the vicious distortions of the Johnson campaign against Barry Goldwater, who was depicted as unstable and trigger-happy.

SHAPING THE MESSAGE

A lot of work had to be done to package this strategy in a convincing way without scaring people or provoking media assault. The development of the strategy evolved slowly over the next few years. It was done in concert, with the work of Peter Hannaford, who bore the important responsibility of working with the governor on the weekly newspaper column and the radio broadcast; Marty Anderson, whose constant counsel on domestic and economic policy was crucial; Ed Meese, whose advice and ability to synopsize Reagan's thoughts were unmatched; Lyn Nofziger, and his masterful operation of the Citizens for the Republic; Dick Wirthlin, with his skillful insights into national public opinion and his capacity to draw strategic conclusions for Reagan; and I, handling the foreign policy and national security aspects. Eventually there were, of course, others who contributed significantly, and not least was William J. Casey, whose contributions began in earnest in early 1980.

As a result, the intellectual and policy components of a national campaign were gradually drawn together. The governor's extensive national speaking schedule was the perfect sounding board to test the themes that emerged. Those themes never varied in the essentials, primarily because he was the principal author of everything he said, and he would never say anything with which he disagreed.

By late 1976, after months of preparation, the Committee on the Present Danger (CPD) was formed. It was an organization of concerned citizens, preponderantly Democrats along with a sprinkling of Republicans, all deeply concerned about the state of our military preparedness and our policy toward the Soviet Union.

As one of the few founding Republican directors of the CPD, I considered it an important counterweight to the prevailing thinking represented by the policy of détente. It was soon obvious that the CPD was moving in the same direction as Governor Reagan, and as the work of the Committee progressed, Reagan joined. The combined resources of the Committee's directors and firepower, including my friends and close colleagues, Fred Iklé and Bill Van Cleave, represented an extraordinary seminar in which Reagan's ideas could be tested and refined.

By 1979 and early 1980, we were holding regular discussions and briefing sessions on both coasts with selected CPD directors, laying the foundation for the bridge over which the neoconservative Democrats could come to the Reagan cause. This is precisely how people such as Paul Nitze, Eugene Rostow, Max Kampelman, Charles Tyroler and, of course, the inimitable and indomitable Jeanne Kirkpatrick and many others made their way ultimately to the Reagan administration.

One cannot overemphasize the importance of this historic coalition. It assisted in the process of Reagan's mastery of subjects such as arms control, military hardware, force structure, budgeting for national security, intelligence capabilities and the like, and assisted him in testing and honing his views on grand strategy.

ENCOUNTER AT THE WALL

There was an obvious need for the governor to embark on foreign travel, and three major trips were planned for 1978.

On the first of April, we visited Japan, Taiwan, and Hong Kong. Leading Japanese were very skeptical about Ronald Reagan. The Taiwanese, on the other hand, were enthusiastic and receptive. It was on this visit that he reaffirmed his determination to preserve Taiwan's integrity and safety.

The second trip was to Britain, France, and Germany, in November 1980. British Prime Minister Callahan declined to meet with the governor, but Margaret Thatcher and Winston Churchill II eagerly did, as did members of the press corps.

In France, President Giscard d'Estaing and Prime Minister Raymond Barre did not have time for Ronald Reagan, and to Reagan's great amusement, we were shunted to an effete third-level snob in the foreign ministry.

Although it is not generally known, until 1978 Ronald Reagan had never set foot in Germany. Chancellor Helmut Schmidt, whom I had known since the 1960s, was wiser than his British and French colleagues; he received us in an extended, but not very warm, meeting. A session with Helmut Kohl, then unknown in the United States, was long and productive, and gave a meaningful head start to the relationship that blossomed once Kohl became chancellor in 1983. In Munich, Reagan met the impressive and influential Franz Joseph Strauss, forming an instant friendship.

It was in Berlin, however, that Reagan experienced a powerful first-hand encounter with the face of communism. Approaching the Berlin Wall, his countenance darkened, and he stood before it in silence for several minutes before turning to Peter Hannaford and me, saying, "We have got to find a way to knock this thing down." Nine years later, as president, he would utter those historic words, "Mr. Gorbachev, tear down this wall."

Entering East Berlin through Checkpoint Charlie, we went to Alexanderplatz and entered a large store. As we departed, we stood on the platz, observing the silent shuffling of the people passing by—no merriment, not much talking, very

drab. At that moment a pair of Volskpolizisten ("People's Police") sauntered past and within thirty feet of us stopped a
citizen carrying shopping bags, forcing him to drop them on
the spot and show his papers, one officer poking him with the
muzzle of an AK-47 and the other probing through the bags
with his gun. I believe the encounter with the wall and witnessing the armed harassment of an ordinary citizen seared
into the governor's memory the brutality of the communist
system, and reinforced his dedication to placing it upon the
ash heap of history.

The third trip, well into the planning stages, was to be to
the Soviet Union, provided there could be a meeting with
Brezhnev. In meetings with then-Ambassador Anatoly Dobrynin, we agreed a meeting could be arranged, but the Kremlin
sent a message through Dobrynin insisting that Reagan not
return to the United States and simply launch an attack.
Clearly, we could not guarantee any outcome. I knew better
than to make a promise that might not be kept, but suggested
to Dobrynin that it would be a good idea to accommodate the
governor since he might see something while there that could
inform his opinion and affect his public policy pronouncements. It was, in any case, to be a quiet, private trip, with no
publicity.

In some ways, this trip could have provided Reagan with
an enormous strategic advantage of an early meeting with the
Soviet leader and the opportunity to discuss his views openly.
Unfortunately, this chance was ruined by an unexpected but
deliberate press leak from John Sears, thus prompting the im-
mediate cancellation of the trip before misunderstanding
among the governor's natural constituency could run out of
control.

THE 1980 PLATFORM:
GUIDE TO GOVERNANCE

The extensive travel here and abroad, the speeches, the articles, the radio broadcasts, and the constant study of critical issues became the amalgam of the 1980 Reagan offensive on foreign affairs and national security. All of this had to be rooted in his particular way of thinking about the revival of the U.S. economy, and were it not for the sorry state of our defenses and the incredible disarray in Carter foreign policy by 1980, foreign policy issues might well have been muted.

Spreading Soviet aggression in Afghanistan, Poland, Central America, and Cuba, hostages in Iran, massive defense and intelligence cuts, and a generally feckless Carter foreign policy catapulted international concerns to a central position in the campaign.

By spring 1980, and especially with the addition of Bill Casey as campaign manager, we began to consider the party platform. We made an important decision to write a platform that would not be focused on winning an election, but rather one that would serve as a guide to action on the very first days of a Reagan administration.

On the foreign policy side, with Fred Iklé, Bill Van Cleave, and Larry Silberman, we formed a large corps of substantive advisers in foreign policy, defense, and intelligence. In this effort, Fred Iklé and Bill Van Cleave each gave a solid year of their lives as volunteers and at zero cost to the campaign. Marty Anderson established a similar corps of advisers on the domestic side. Of the 120 advisers who worked with us over long months, virtually each one had the opportunity to meet with and brief the candidate, and their work was integrated into the campaign.

By early 1980, few inside the Beltway believed Ronald Reagan could be a serious candidate. Losing in Iowa galvanized the governor, and he decided to campaign in his own style, barnstorming through New Hampshire by bus day after day, morning, noon, and night. Resting his campaign on straight-forward notions reflected in a platform that was entitled simply "Family, Neighborhood, Work, Peace, and Freedom," he directed that no statement, no release, no speech be made without complete conformity with those five fundamental concepts.

Earlier I referred to the unanimity among the group working closely with Reagan. That unity and purpose of vision was, in my mind, absolutely crucial to the smooth campaign that brought final victory. Inevitably, a postconvention campaign brings new people and a great deal of posturing and backstabbing. Yet there was very little of this in 1980 and none detectable at the upper reaches. That would change, of course, when the election was over, but the single vision prevailed throughout the fall.

PEOPLE ARE POLICY

Better than anyone, Ronald Reagan knew that policy does not exist as an abstract notion; to implement it, the right people are indispensable. As he put it, "Surround yourself with the best people you can find, delegate authority, and do not interfere as long as the policy you have decided upon is being carried out." Thus it was that a large reservoir of skilled people who had participated in the campaign were ready for action on Day One of the new administration.

The first year of the administration was replete with examples of Reagan's determination to implement his plan. There was a leader, and the leader had a clear concept of how to marshal U.S. strength in the service of a historic objective.

As he had remarked to me in January 1977, his overriding objective was to assure that we would win and they would lose; this was at once a prophecy and a plan. That he succeeded beyond our expectations and his own, and those of the rest of the world, is both a matter of record and the main event of the second half of the twentieth century.

3

"The World Is Our Oyster"

MEETING THE SOVIET MILITARY CHALLENGE

Fred C. Iklé

I FIND IT DAUNTING to talk to this group and say anything new. You know the events we are discussing, and many, many of you were key participants. Therefore, I will focus on one or two episodes you may not remember so well and then draw some lessons that ought to be stressed because of all the muddled ideas on foreign policy that are now circulating in Washington.

First, some hard data: U.S. defense spending grew from the $134 billion in the last Carter year to $282 billion in the seventh Reagan year, more than doubling. The election in November 1980 had, of course, provided the political energy that made this possible.

This wholesome impulse from the electorate, as Cap Weinberger realized right away, had to be exploited quickly. We in the Pentagon had to lead with a big defense budget increase, because in later years Congress would become more opposed. For choosing the right tactic, credit should also go to Bill Schneider, who was then in charge of defense at the Office of Management and Budget (OMB). I remember well the day we met in Cap Weinberger's office in the Pentagon, preparing the supplemental request to be sent to the OMB, when Bill knew all the ins and outs of budget-making and steered us to the winning number.

THE SS-20 CHALLENGE

Another far-reaching intervention by the Pentagon at that time concerned arms control, specifically the negotiations and intermediate nuclear forces in Europe, the so-called INF. You will recall that the Soviet Union had already started deploying a large number of their SS-20 missiles threatening NATO Europe, and they were deploying more month after month.

The Carter administration in its own way sought to cope with this threat. It made an agreement with NATO allies, the so-called two-track approach, stating that NATO should prepare for the deployment in Europe of our countervailing missiles but should start to negotiate with Moscow for an arms control solution.

Predictably, the Europeans wanted to move ahead on negotiations and hold back on deployment. The State Department as well wanted to charge ahead with negotiations. Meanwhile, noisy demonstrations took place all over Europe against our deployment of the countervailing missiles (demonstrations that recently released Soviet documents reveal were stirred up by the KGB).

Here, then, was the predicament for our Reagan team on this issue in 1981: One, the Carter administration had committed the United States to negotiations. Two, the Soviets had already deployed a large number of missiles and kept adding new ones every month. Three, NATO's countervailing deployment had not yet even started, and faced strong pacifist opposition in Europe. Four, the State Department came up with one idea after another for concessions to Moscow.

Happily, at that time, Cap Weinberger's Pentagon was no shrinking violet in the foreign policy arena. Our motto was: "The world is our oyster." And over the next eight years, we ate that oyster.

Credit for cracking the oyster shell pertaining to the SS-20 Soviet missiles belongs to my good friend, Richard Perle, who was my deputy at that time. He invented the winning tactic, the zero-zero deal whereby the Soviets had to get rid of all of their SS-20 missiles, down to zero, and we would get rid of our countervailing missiles.

Cap Weinberger immediately saw the great advantage of this deal and became its victorious advocate. The advantage was that, first, zero-zero would catch the European pacifists in their own trap, for what could be more pacifist than abolishing all these missiles? We thus forced the European pacifists to argue, "No, we must deploy some missiles to accommodate the Russian deployments," and that was hard for them to do. Second, the Soviets, by opposing the zero option, would show their intention was to achieve nuclear domination over Europe.

The whole deal had a cunning simplicity—but the State Department hated it. Happily, Richard Allen and Ed Meese saw to it that President Reagan got Weinberger's recommendation before the interagency process had turned it into chopped salad.

Reagan loved it. It became the U.S. position despite ridicule in the media and the Congress, and despite sabotage among some U.S. diplomats.

Zero-zero led to the destruction of this formidable Soviet

missile force, and it allowed us in the United States to strengthen and deploy our nuclear deterrent more effectively than by inserting missiles among European towns and villages.

I have given more time to this one example of Reagan's policy-making because it has received less attention in the histories of this period. More importantly, it directly and personally involved President Reagan and therefore tells us a great deal about his profound comprehension of our nation's security needs.

Reagan understood far better than all the strategic technicians and arms control experts the deep flaws of mutual assured destruction (MAD). This is why he chose to move forward so boldly on the Strategic Defense Initiative (SDI)—to make nuclear missiles "impotent and obsolete." This is why he liked the zero-zero option so much—to get rid of a whole class of Soviet missiles, instead of adding another layer of missiles to perpetuate MAD. It is this larger and deeper understanding of our long-term interests that gave Reagan the inner strength and the credibility to convince Gorbachev that SDI was not a bargaining chip but that all the intermediate range missiles could and should be dismantled.

By the way, the better and brighter Russians have since admitted that Reagan was right all along. By contrast, those U.S. academics and journalists who were proven so wrong in their harsh criticism of Reagan's approach to Moscow have never had the decency and honesty to admit their error about the Cold War. Isn't it noteworthy that one can find more honesty today among Russian academics than among left-wing U.S. academics?

WHAT KEPT THE COLD WAR GOING

Essential for bringing the Cold War to an end was the Reagan administration's concentration on what kept the Cold War going. What kept it going was neither some superficial misunderstanding between East and West, nor a shortage of arms control treaties. It was instead the continued existence of the "evil empire" that kept the Cold War going. Ronald Reagan had the courage to articulate what was then an incendiary idea but is now a hackneyed truth; namely, that we had a Cold War because of the evil empire, and could not end the Cold War without undoing that empire.

From this realization flowed the whole game plan. We had to bend every effort to undo the Soviet empire. The Reagan Defense Department did not merely deploy better tanks in the Fulda Gap or new Trident missiles for the MAD strategy. No, together with Bill Casey's CIA we fought on every front:

- We pushed ahead with SDI.
- We throttled the leakage of technology to the Soviet military.
- We used our leverage with our allies to curtail Soviet gas sales to Europe.
- We supported Savimbi in Angola.
- We armed the Freedom Fighters in Nicaragua.
- We helped the Salvadoran military to protect free elections.
- We supported Radio Marti against Fidel Castro.
- We liberated Grenada.

- We put Stinger missiles into Afghanistan to shoot down Soviet aircraft.

Overall, we never accepted the notion that we ought to *stabilize* the Soviet Union.

A DIFFERENT APPROACH TODAY

Mark the contrast with today. In the 1980s, by destabilizing the Soviet Union, we dealt with the *causes* of the Cold War, not its symptoms. And we won. Today, a mini-Cold War is left over from the big one; namely, the confrontation in Korea that keeps the peninsula divided, threatens the peace in Northeast Asia, and imprisons the people in the North with utter cruelty. The Clinton administration, however, instead of seeking to undo the evil North Korean dictatorship, strives to stabilize and propitiate North Korea by giving it expensive new reactors, by donating fuel and food for the North Korean military, and by pleading for peace negotiations that would merely whitewash and consolidate that dictatorship.

Since this symposium is in honor of Bill Casey, I want to close with a thought inspired by him. His lifetime work taught us

- that wisdom without courage cannot lead
- and that courage without wisdom will lead us astray.

Bill always strove for the best possible information and understanding of the world, and then he made this rich knowledge useful for our nation by bringing to bear his great personal courage.

Now, what does that have do to with the end of the Cold

War? We do have knowledge all right; we know a great deal about today's complicated world. The raw U.S. intelligence collection seems pretty good. For example, the raw data about the spread of missile technology is at hand, although it required the Rumsfeld Commission to give it meaning. Plenty of data proving Iraq's cheating on arms control has been gathered, thanks to Ambassador Butler's leadership of UNSCOM and intrepid analysts like Scott Ritter. Our government has other vast and valuable intelligence collections, perhaps more than during Bill Casey's time. To act in the complex world since the end of the Cold War, we don't lack knowledge. We lack leaders like Bill Casey who have the courage to give strategic meaning to what we know.

4

NSDD-75

A NEW APPROACH
TO THE SOVIET UNION

William P. Clark

THIS IS THE FIRST OCCASION I have had in sixteen years to talk about this subject. One of the benefits of coming toward the end of the line today is that I can cut my remarks down and avoid duplication from what we have heard from our good speakers thus far.

Nineteen eighty-one gave President Reagan and his team the opportunity, quoting him, to get his "domestic house in order," which he did, after facing double-digit inflation, interest rates, and unemployment upon entering office.

At the end of 1981 he called us into the Oval Office and said, "Gentlemen, our concentration has been on domestic matters this year, and I want to roll the sleeves up now and get to foreign policy, defense, and intelligence," beginning the first week of January 1982. And he said, "By the way, lean on our experience in Sacramento. Take a leaf from our book out there in our decision-making process, if we would, and let's get moving."

THE REAGAN NATIONAL SECURITY PROCESS

The national security process began with morning meetings, briefings, as the president's daily brief, the famous PDB, prepared by Bill Casey and his team through the night, preceding my 9 o'clock Oval Office briefing. That frequently got to the president before he came down from the residence, and by then he had penciled in comments for follow-up by Bill and the Agency during the day.

Furthermore, we started the process of NSDDs, National Security Decision Directives. Let me explain to those of you who may not be familiar with those designations. Again, in January of 1982, under the direction of Tom Reed, we began, at the president's direction, the study of the overall Soviet situation and what our existing relations were and what they should be.

The earlier study directive became a continuum, a process up through the first two years, in which the crafted studies would be led primarily by the State Department, recognizing the sensitivities of prior NSC's taking the lead away from CIA, Defense, and State.

These study directives developed into decision directives, from number 2 up to 120, in that period of time, and these studies and resulting decision directives were important from the standpoint of creating the national security policy for President Reagan and his administration.

NSDD-75

As Dick Allen and others have said, Ronald Reagan arrived in Washington with a clear vision, with a clear philosophy that had been developed over many years, and the question arose, "How do we convert that vision, that foresight into policy, policy into strategy, strategy into tactics?" And thus we come to NSDD-75 in December of 1982.

I would like to describe part of the covering memo, again borrowing a page from our Sacramento days. The president liked short foundational memos—four paragraphs if possible: the issue, facts, discussion with the alternatives, and finally the recommendations of the National Security Council members.

The covering letter to the president in December followed a year's study by every agency involved: State, Defense, CIA, Treasury, the Attorney General, Commerce, OMB, the U.N. Ambassador's office, the Joint Chiefs, United States Information Agency, Energy, U.S. Trade Representative, and the Arms Control Disarmament Agency—all participated and signed off. Not that the president was kept in the dark during these studies; he was continually briefed on projects.

My covering memo stated that U.S. policy toward the Soviet Union would consist of three elements: first, external resistance to Soviet imperialism; second, internal pressure on the USSR to weaken the sources of Soviet imperialism; and third, negotiations to eliminate, on the basis of strict reciprocity, outstanding disagreements.

We emphasized the second of these objectives. Internal pressure on the USSR represented a new objective of U.S. policy.

A NEW APPROACH TO THE SOVIET UNION

It has always been the objective of U.S. policy toward the Soviet Union to combine containment with negotiations, but the attached document to the covering memo was the first in which the United States Government added a third objective to its relations with the Soviet Union; namely, encouraging antitotalitarian changes within the USSR and refraining from assisting the Soviet regime to consolidate further its hold on the country.

The basic premise behind this new approach was that it made little sense to seek to stop Soviet imperialism externally while helping to strengthen the regime internally. This objective was to be attained by a combination of economic and ideological instrumentalities.

Thus it became United States policy to avoid subsidizing the Soviet economy or unduly easing the burden of Soviet resource allocation decisions, so as not to dilute pressures for structural change within the Soviet system.

In the ideological competition, the United States would strongly affirm the superiority of Western values, expose the double standards employed by the Soviet Union in dealing with difficulties within its own domain and the outside world, and prevent the Soviet Union from seizing the semantic high ground in the battle of ideas. The United States should in addition seek to weaken Moscow's hold on its empire.

This was difficult language for some in the bureaucracy. Agriculture, Commerce, State—all had difficulty with the new internal pressures approach.

First of all, there was disparity among our intelligence agencies as to just how weak the Soviets were internally. Some felt the Soviet economy was quite strong, but Reagan decided we would take the chance on assisting their destabilization.

Richard Pipes and John Lenczowski, of the NSC staff, warned us in the first days of the administration that never had the Soviets been a greater threat for the simple reason that the Kremlin had reached the conclusion that they had military superiority, both nuclear and conventional, to start and win the war against us.

Dr. Pipes went on to add, and things shook among some staff in the White House, that war was inevitable unless we were able to change the Soviet system.

Frankly, there were enough of us who believed that to be the case, and, thus, we worked hard on that new policy element of trying to turn the Soviet Union inside itself. And of course, that did occur.

Dr. Pipes also noticed, following our several addresses announcing this new approach, that the Soviets were frightened by it. They did not even mention it, publicly. They called us the usual adventurous warmongers, but did not mention the new element that we had placed in our policy of attempting to go to their inside in changing the hearts and minds, not necessarily of the Soviet leadership, but at least of their people.

The NSDD process continued beyond number 75 and included setting up the three Liberty radio stations, the Office of Public Diplomacy, and working on other aspects of public diplomacy.

COALITION BUILDING

Another process the president asked us to use, again taking a page from our Sacramento days, was to reach out to others on a bipartisan basis to get the support that we would need from the Congress and from the people. We developed such things as the Kissinger Commission, in which Jeanne Kirkpatrick was heavily involved, to try to look at Central America—

not only at security issues, but also the longer-term social issues.

We created, furthermore, the Commission on Strategic
Forces, which included Brent Scowcroft, Nick Brady, Al Haig,
Richard Helms, and others, who were effective in meeting the
nuclear freeze movement that was very serious not only in
attacking our efforts in arms control but also in opposing our
defense budget.

These two and other commissions were both bipartisan
and effective. At times, we were criticized for reaching outside
to the significant people from prior administrations and from
the other party, but the approach was effective.

Other changes that President Reagan brought into being,
in contrast to prior administrations, included a standing
scheduled meeting with the Joint Chiefs of Staff and their
great leader, Jack Vessey. He arrived in 1982 and was very significant in leadership, particularly in the INF effort and mod-
ernization of our NATO and nuclear forces in Europe.

REAGAN AND REVISIONISM

Let me go on to this revisionism effort that seems to be of
such concern—that asks whether the Reagan administration
is receiving its due credit for bringing down the Berlin Wall.

If we can mention again the president's favorite admonition, his Cabinet in 1981 at Christmas received an etched
piece of crystal, which said, "You can accomplish anything if
you don't worry about who gets the credit." If he were here to
comment on what is going on in academia today, he would tell
us, again, not to worry about it. And he would also add another
favorite saying of his, "The truth always rises to the surface.
We can hear that in every language."

Thus, I think we should take that leaf and recognize that

in his courage and selflessness, he never wanted to take credit for anything. I once heard someone say, "Congratulations, Mr. President, on your success in ending the Cold War." He smiled and said, "No, not my success but a team effort by divine providence."

REAGAN AND THE DIGNITY OF HUMAN LIFE

In describing the superpower competition, President Reagan rarely used the term "Cold War." He called it a "conflict." I truly believe that in the time that we were together in Sacramento, and later in Washington, all of us realized his love of life—and not just life at the moment, but all human life.

He always took occasion in his major addresses to mention the sanctity and the dignity of human life. This was again brought to the attention of more than one person upon his seeing the gruesome SIOP presentations in the Situation Room, in which scenarios were laid out for how a nuclear war might be fought. He would watch that screen showing the worst of possibilities of nuclear war, watch the red marks spread as the bomb drops occurred in the Soviet Union as well as on our own population, to really see America destroyed. All eyes glared at him at times as he bit the lower lip, and the question arose: Would he, if necessity came, be able as commander in chief to give that terrible order?

When John Vessey became Chairman of the Joint Chiefs, he asked me that question, "Would our commander in chief be able to act?"

Remember, we never said "no first strike." When the president was asked by a reporter, "Would we ever strike the Soviets first?" he answered, "The president never says never."

I said to Jack Vessey, "Jack, that is a question that you are going to have to ask the president himself." I told the president the Chairman of the Joint Chiefs wanted to come in with that question, and the president said, "Fine, Bill."

I remember, I took a chair and he pulled it up to the front of the desk and said, "Mr. President, can you?" And the president said, "Absolutely, if it becomes necessary. I have taken the oath of office to protect our people, and the first duty of government is survival of its people." But he would continue to remind us of the sanctity and dignity of human life and our duty to protect it.

The "evil empire" speech that we have all heard so much about was not so much about the Soviet Union as it was about Ronald Reagan. It was condemned by so many people, but to many of us it was probably his greatest speech because it was so much the real Ronald Reagan.

He, I think, will be remembered by those of us who worked with him in Sacramento and in Washington as being far wiser than his Cabinet and his staff combined. I will never forget Ambassdor Dobrynin saying, "We worry about President Reagan, we don't necessarily like him, but he is the one world leader that is totally predictable, and while he may vary his strategy and tactics, he will never vary his principles." Of course, that courageous person is the man who led us to the victory we are celebrating today.

5

Rollback

INTELLIGENCE AND THE REAGAN STRATEGY IN THE DEVELOPING WORLD

Edwin Meese III

I SEE SO MANY PEOPLE in the audience who had a major part in the events that we talk about today that it is almost embarrassing to come before you and not have a roomful of people participating in a seminar rather than having this talk. But it is great to see how many people here today had such a part in the successes of the Reagan administration and the ultimate result of victory in the Cold War.

I have been given three missions: first, to talk about the intelligence situation during the Reagan administration; secondly, to talk a little about the Reagan policies as they pertain to the Third World; and thirdly, to briefly compare the Reagan approach to national security with the situation that pertains today.

THE PROBLEM WITH INTELLIGENCE

To get a little bit of a perspective on how things were in 1980, to fully appreciate the policy changes that brought an end to the Cold War, it is important to look back at the situation that Ronald Reagan faced when he took office on the 21st of January in 1981. It is hard to remember in some way how bad things were, particularly in the national security field.

We had an underfunded military at the time. There were serious questions about whether the military could be properly used with the syndrome from Vietnam still hanging over us.

In terms of foreign policy, we had an acquiescence to virtually perpetual coexistence with the Soviet Union, and an acceptance of the inevitable continuance, if not triumph, of socialism as an economic doctrine, and Marxist totalitarianism as a political doctrine.

Bleak as that was, the intelligence situation was not much better. Indeed, it was perhaps even worse.

During the 1970s we had the Church Committee in Congress, which had disastrously revealed intelligence sources and methods to the probable destruction of many of our agents overseas and certainly to the debilitation of our intelligence resources. That was followed up by a policy in the late 1970s in which some 700 key agents were dismissed through retirement or firing in one fell swoop, thus cutting out and disrupting agent networks throughout the world, destroying confidence in our intelligence system, and certainly making it virtually impossible to recruit new agents in those foreign countries to take their place.

That was why Ronald Reagan, in probably the first or second decision he made on personnel in 1980, told Bill Casey that he wanted him to be the director of Central Intelligence.

The president-elect was very aware of what Bill had done during World War II as the head of secret intelligence in Europe and the tremendous job he had done in bringing success to the Office of Strategic Services (OSS).

He called upon Bill to do that job, even though Bill himself, given his choice, probably would have preferred one or two other jobs within the administration. He had already done intelligence—but he had expertise that Ronald Reagan badly needed and, as Bill always did when called upon to serve his country, he took the job. He accomplished a great deal and did a terrific job as Reagan's director of Central Intelligence.

He revitalized the intelligence community not just in terms of getting adequate funding, not just in terms of organization and setting up the structures, but also in making sure his staff knew they had his support, his encouragement, and his leadership, as well as that of the commander in chief.

One of the things that Bill brought to intelligence was something he had learned during World War II, and that was not just the importance of collecting intelligence, but also the importance of intelligence analysis. He believed in competitive analysis, so that the policymakers who were going to use this information had the best results of a variety of people looking at the same situation, even though they might have conflicting views. He believed the president needed to have the benefit of that kind of thinking.

He also was very good in making sure that sound intelligence was translated into a usable basis for policymaking and decisions. As the director of Central Intelligence and as a valued member of the National Security Council, he gave the president excellent advice, particularly on things such as the Third World.

It was a great team, with Bill Casey knowing how to produce the intelligence and Ronald Reagan knowing how to use it.

THE REAGAN STRATEGY

To understand our success in the Cold War, I think it is important to recognize the importance of the overall Reagan strategy. The U.S. military buildup during that period of time and the economic constraints that were imposed on the Soviet Union have already been explored in detail by other panelists.

I would like to mention three other parts of the strategy that have been at least alluded to, but will talk about them a little more because they are important elements of the strategy.

The first, of course, was to engage the Soviet Union on a moral level. Naturally one thinks immediately of the "evil empire" speech, but that was only part of what Ronald Reagan had been saying. Certainly he felt that totalitarianism and oppression were wrong from a moral standpoint—but he also felt they had the seeds of their own destruction.

That is why in 1982, speaking to the British Parliament in Westminster, he talked about consigning communism to the ash heap of history.

I think most of my colleagues here would agree with me that even Ronald Reagan, as optimistic as he was when he made that statement in June of 1982, did not think it would happen as quickly as it did. But he was absolutely sure that it would happen, and that confidence underlay all the policies that he established during his term in office.

The second major part of the strategy was the fact that he was determined to halt the aggression of the Soviet Union. Indeed, during his term of office, there was not one square kilometer of new soil that fell beneath the boots of Soviet troops.

The third and perhaps most important aspect of the strategy was President Reagan's determination to roll back the prior aggression through support of Freedom Fighters around the world.

The Soviets had worked long and hard on taking over the Third World. They had taken its leaders and brought them to Moscow where they indoctrinated the indigenous leadership of many countries and gave them both the philosophy and the tools to spread Marxism into their nations.

The president's views, echoing information provided by Bill Casey, rested on two important tenets. First, that Marxism had failed to liberate less-developed countries, and in fact had wrought misery, famine, and genocide of historic proportions. Second, that the United States in the 1980s had a unique opportunity to help oppressed peoples resist totalitarian regimes and to inject free-market ideas into less developed countries so they would truly secure freedom and opportunity.

One of the countries that he particularly staked out for this was Nicaragua, which had been the classic blueprint for Soviet-style oppression. The president believed that it was a pivotal test of U.S. resolve to fan new flames of freedom in the Third World.

Bill Casey contributed greatly to both the intelligence and the policy that developed into a winning strategy in the Third World. Casey had given many speeches on this in the early days as Central Intelligence director, both inside the administration and outside, and expressed his concern about human rights and, for strategic reasons, about Soviet imperialism that was creeping into the Third World.

In one speech, he said that in a mere ten years the number of Warsaw Pact and Cuban troops, military advisers, and technicians stationed in Third World countries had increased an incredible 500 percent.

He went on to say they had expanded their reach to a number of countries near the strategic choke points of the West, including the Panama Canal, the Straits of Gibraltar, the Suez Canal, the Straits of Hormuz, the entrance to the Red Sea, and from Cam Rahn Bay in Vietnam to the sea lanes of East Asia.

Elsewhere, Bill Casey said, Marxist-Leninist policies and tactics had unleashed the four horsemen of the apocalypse: famine, pestilence, war, and death.

He went on to list the countries that were involved. Countries such as Afghanistan, Angola, and Cambodia were kept under Marxist control by more than 300,000 Soviet, Cuban, and Vietnamese troops. Half a dozen other countries—Ethiopia, Nicaragua, South Yemen, Cuba, and Vietnam—were controlled by committed Marxist-Leninist governments with military and population control assistance from the Soviet bloc.

Most of the other countries in the Third World were suffering some degree of stagnation, impoverishment, or famine.

This was the background to developing a strategy for dealing with the Third World. It was a strategy that involved supporting Freedom Fighters. It involved assisting economic forces in countries that were trying to develop new free market methods of operating. It combined a variety of military, diplomatic, and economic initiatives in order to change things in the Third World.

AFGHANISTAN AND NICARAGUA

Time does not allow a country-by-country analysis, but I think there are two examples that are particularly important. The first is Afghanistan, where Soviet troops had marched in during the late 1970s. The Reagan administration provided the

Freedom Fighters all kinds of weapons, tactical assistance, and training, along with encouragement to resist Soviet aggression.

Perhaps the most important decision that was made was to give them advanced antiaircraft weapons, including the Stinger missile, which was really the decision that broke the back of the Soviet army. Suddenly these guerrillas, these Freedom Fighters, were able to bring down Soviet aircraft and make it virtually impossible for them to use their most effective weapon—namely, using air superiority to control the country.

In Central America, when President Reagan took office in 1981, El Salvador was in tremendous jeopardy of being overrun by insurrectionist forces that were being fueled, trained, led, and guided by the Marxist forces in Nicaragua.

The support and assistance given to Freedom Fighters in Nicaragua had two results: to make it impossible for Nicaraguan Marxists to support the insurgency in El Salvador and at the same time to start the forces of democracy working in Nicaragua itself.

The results in these two cases are clear. The Red Army was defeated in Afghanistan. In Central America El Salvador is safe from communist domination and Nicaragua is now a democracy rather than a second bastion of Marxism in our own hemisphere.

YESTERDAY AND TODAY

What then is the comparison with what is going on today in our country and what went on during those eight years that changed the world?

Today, unfortunately, our national security apparatus is in the hands of many of the people who contributed to the problems in the 1970s that Ronald Reagan had to correct in the 1980s.

These are the people who were wrong about the 1980s, including such people as Strobe Talbott, who has moved from pundit to policymaker. These are the people who are responsible for foreign and defense policies and practices that have jeopardized our security, have violated principles of integrity and consistency, and have failed to keep faith, particularly with the men and women in our armed forces who have the ultimate mission of protecting our citizens and our country. We have to remember if we analyze who is there: the State Department today is being led by Jimmy Carter's third string.

There is no way that people who cannot learn the lessons of victory that Ronald Reagan taught will ever learn how to effectively provide us with a national security policy that will advance our interest, keep us out of situations and places where we do not belong, and ultimately contribute to world peace and stability on a rational basis.

Today, our military situation is in great jeopardy. Our national defense is being undermined in three ways. First, by a lack of funding and budgetary support for our armed forces. Training is down and spare parts are running low because the funding is simply not there. Funding is also an important reason why our recruiting and retention goals are not being met. Hundreds, if not thousands, of very capable, very dedicated men and women are leaving the services because, on the one hand, many of them cannot afford to stay and, on the other hand, many of them are demoralized by some of the things they see happening.

Second, we have a deployment policy and operating tempos that are straining the armed forces. These deployments are keeping people away from their families for long periods of time because we have inadequate numbers of forces and ships.

The Clinton administration is deploying our forces in unprecedented situations never before deemed to be part of our national interest. We have, in short, fewer resources, but more deployments.

Finally, we have the social engineering that is occurring in the armed forces. It began in the first days of the new administration in 1993 when an attempt was made to change the traditional policies related to homosexuals in the military, and more recently the policies pertaining to women in combat. These detrimental policies, imposed by an administration of people who openly talked about "loathing" the military, have had a corrosive effect on the morale of the people who join our armed forces. Our soldiers joined to serve their country. Our soldiers joined to serve their country and to become warriors in defense of our nation, not to be products of social engineering.

In intelligence, the disdain for effective intelligence and a reluctance to properly fund it leave us without the necessary capacity at a time when intelligence is needed more than it ever was before, certainly as much or perhaps even more than during the Cold War. We need effective intelligence today because during the Cold War, at least we knew who our adversaries were and where the trouble spots might be.

Today, we have all types of situations around the world where we have trouble knowing when trouble might appear. This is partially because of the lack of intelligence capability, partially because of the unknowable intentions of leaders in many of those countries, and partially because of instability in regions such as the Korean peninsula and the Middle East.

To demonstrate how unpredictable the post–Cold War world can be, I give you the example of the Persian Gulf. In 1988, we probably would have gotten 100-to-1 odds that three years later we would not be fighting a war in the Persian Gulf, at least against Iraq. And yet it happened. A similar situation can happen again today as we have a variety of rulers and situations in the world that make intelligence important in itself. This is even more true with the reduced capabilities of our armed forces. We need the lead time necessary to move our people into the proper places in order to contend with future trouble spots.

With intelligence, as in foreign and defense policy, our nation can best correct today's dismal situation by reading and heeding the lessons of the Reagan years that led to the winning of the Cold War.

6

Lessons to be Learned
. . . and Applied

Frank J. Gaffney Jr.

UNLIKE THE OTHER FOLKS on this dais, I was a genuinely bit player in the Reagan effort that has been described here so magnificently.

Having said that, my years in the Reagan administration were the happiest and I think the most personally gratifying years of my life. Second only to the satisfaction I associate with that period is the pleasure of being back with so many of these people and hearing from them the authentic story of how the Cold War was won.

It is my privilege, as well as my duty, to turn the last few minutes of this conversation from the retrospective to the prospective—to assess where we go from here, given the lessons that are there to be learned.

What can we do to ensure that the principles that brought us great success in the past are once again permitted to be—

indeed, made a necessary part of—our security policies, both today and tomorrow?

I would like to start by saying that I think one of the most ineluctable aspects of this effort must be to learn about and to understand just what made these successes possible.

What you have heard here today is an oral history, one that I found particularly powerful. We need to teach this history. It is not enough for those of us who had the honor of being part of it to remember it and share anecdotally some of our insights. It must be conveyed to future generations. Otherwise we risk having the Cold War be the first war in history whose story is being written by the losers. That is clearly an unacceptable situation.

I want to personally salute people like the Hoover Institution's Peter Schweizer, Sven Kraemer, and my friend, John Lenczowski of the Institute of World Politics, Dick Scaife, the Casey family, and others in this room and elsewhere who are making available to the next generation this sort of historical education rooted in the facts.

It is certainly the case, as Judge Clark noted, that President Reagan believed that truth must rise to the surface, but I think we all have to do our part to ensure that it gets there.

I would also argue that we must organize to restore the Reagan-era principles, which have been discussed so well this afternoon, to their proper place as the structure underpinning U.S security policy.

I will summarize them—it does not do justice to them—as at least fivefold.

The first is clearly the principle of peace through strength.

The second is the abiding commitment to individual freedom and economic opportunity not only here at home but also around the world.

The third, an indispensable ingredient of both of the other

two, is the necessity for credible, competent, and steadfast U.S. leadership in international affairs.

I urge you to think about how far we have strayed from those principles as we look at the debacles unfolding as we speak in Kosovo, Iraq, Russia, China, North Korea, and elsewhere.

I would be so bold as to suggest building upon some of the points that Dick Allen has made: Now is the time for a new Committee on the Present Danger because the present danger is back, and we need a mechanism that will bring together people like those in this room, and many across this great country and, for that matter, around the world who share a common commitment to these principles.

I can say on behalf of the Center for Security Policy that we certainly will be prepared to do our part to facilitate the organization and the operation of such an effort if it can be mounted. And I urge you all to participate, not least because there is an important—I think, in fact, necessary—political aspect to all of this at the moment. We must arouse the public. And we must engage their elected representatives, including, of course, those who would be president of this country, by holding them accountable for making sound security policies a preeminent part of the national agenda.

If we fail to do this, let there be no doubt, it is not going to come out right. The best I think we can hope for is that we find ourselves once again up against some terrible struggle, twilight or otherwise, and the difference may be this time around that the conflict will be a come-as-you-are party, not one for which we have the opportunity to prepare ourselves properly.

A fourth principle is that we must understand the growing importance of the nexus between U.S. national security and international economic, financial, and technology developments. This is, of course, a trend that Bill Casey foresaw and addressed with extraordinary, if all too characteristic, acumen.

We must ensure that this nexus, too, is properly understood, and that U.S. policies governing this area give due weight to national security concerns, not just expedient, parochial, and often extremely shortsighted business interests.

Fifth and finally, we must implement at long last Ronald Reagan's single most important national security initiative, by beginning to deploy an effective antimissile system capable of ending our current abject and reckless vulnerability to attack.

For twenty-seven years now, since the signing of the ABM treaty in 1972—and sadly for the sixteen long years since President Reagan in March of 1983 gave his speech outlining SDI—we have seen first the Soviets and then the Russians keep the United States in a posture of assured vulnerability, thanks to their advocates and apologists in our own country. I think it is self-evident that this is a posture with which we literally can no longer live.

So let us go forward from this room not only moved by what we remember from these glorious years of old, but committed to bringing to the years ahead the kind of safety, the kind of opportunity, both personal and national, that gave Ronald Reagan's era its leitmotiv as the shining city on a hill and an inspiration to the world at large.

THE PARTICIPANTS

RICHARD V. ALLEN is a Senior Fellow at the Hoover Institution and an international business consultant in Washington, D.C. Mr. Allen served as National Security Adviser to President Reagan during the first year of his administration. From 1977 to 1980 Mr. Allen was Reagan's Chief Foreign Policy Adviser. Mr. Allen was Deputy Assistant to the President of the United States and Deputy Executive Director of the Council on International Economic Policy at the White House from 1971 to 1972. In 1968, Mr. Allen was Chief Foreign Policy Coordinator for the campaign of Richard Nixon, and was later appointed Senior Staff member of the National Security Council.

WILLIAM P. CLARK is Chief Executive Officer of Clark Company and serves as Senior Counsel to the law firm of Clark, Cali, and Negranti. He earlier served as United States Secretary of Interior, Adviser to the President for National Security

Affairs, Deputy Secretary of State, and Chief of Staff to Governor Ronald Reagan. Following completion of eighteen years of full-time public service, Mr. Clark was appointed by President Reagan to serve as Chairman of the Task Group on Nuclear Weapons Program Management (the Packard Commission) and as a member of the Defense Department's Commission on Integrated Long-Term Strategy. Mr. Clark is a Trustee of the Ronald Reagan Presidential Foundation and Library.

FRANK J. GAFFNEY JR. is the Founder and President of the Center for Security Policy in Washington, D.C. Mr. Gaffney acted as Assistant Secretary of Defense for International Security Policy during the Reagan administration, following four years of service as Deputy Assistant Secretary of Defense for Nuclear Forces and Arms Control Policy. Mr. Gaffney had previously served as a Professional Staff Member on the Senate Armed Forces Committee under the chairmanship of the late Senator John Tower. Prior to joining the Committee, Mr. Gaffney was for four years on the staff of the late Senator Henry M. Jackson.

FRED C. IKLÉ is a Distinguished Scholar at the Center for Strategic and International Studies. Mr. Iklé was Under Secretary of Defense for Policy in the Reagan administration and served Presidents Nixon and Ford as Director of the U.S. Arms Control and Disarmament Agency. He served as Chairman of the Republican National Committee's Advisory Council on International Security and as Coordinator of Governor Ronald Reagan's Foreign Policy Advisers. Mr. Iklé has held positions with the Social Science Department of the RAND Corporation, the Center for International Affairs at Harvard University, and the Bureau of Applied Social Research at Columbia University.

EDWIN MEESE III holds the Ronald Reagan Chair in Public Policy at the Heritage Foundation, a Washington-based public policy research and education institution. He is also a Distinguished Visiting Fellow at the Hoover Institution. Mr. Meese served as the 75th Attorney General of the United States from February 1985 to August 1988. From January 1981 to February 1985, Mr. Meese held the position of Counselor to the President, the senior position on the White House Staff, where he functioned as President Reagan's chief policy adviser. As Attorney General and Counselor, Mr. Meese was a member of the President's Cabinet and the National Security Council.

ROGER W. ROBINSON JR. (moderator) is Chair of the William J. Casey Institute and President of RWR, Inc., a Washington-based consulting firm that specializes in advancing "national interest" transactions and projects internationally. Prior to forming his consulting firm, Mr. Robinson was Senior Director of International Economic Affairs at the National Security Council. Prior to joining the NSC staff, Mr. Robinson was a Vice President in the International Department of the Chase Manhattan Bank in New York City. As a banker, he had responsibilities for Chase's loan portfolio to the USSR, Eastern Europe, and Yugoslavia. He also served as a personal staff assistant to former Chase Chairman David Rockefeller.

PETER SCHWEIZER is a research fellow at the Hoover Institution and a best-selling author. Mr. Schweizer is the author of *Victory: The Reagan Administration's Secret Strategy That Hastened the Collapse of the Soviet Union* (Atlantic Monthly Press). A history of the Cold War based on exclusive interviews with U.S. cabinet-level officers as well as officials of the

Soviet KGB, Central Committee, and Politburo, *Victory* was nominated for the Pulitzer Prize and has been published in seven languages. His written work has also appeared in *Foreign Affairs*, *The New York Times*, and *The Wall Street Journal*.